EYE-WITNESSES TO IRELAND IN REVOLT

EYE- WITNESSES TO HISTORY *EDITED BY JAMES HEWITT*

Eye-Witnesses to Nelson's Battles
Eye-Witnesses to the Indian Mutiny
Eye-Witnesses to Wagon Trains West
Eye-Witnesses to Ireland in Revolt
Eye-Witnesses to the English Civil War

Eye-Witnesses to Ireland in Revolt

Edited by James Hewitt

 OSPREY PUBLISHING LTD

First published in 1974 by
Osprey Publishing Ltd, P.O. Box 25,
707 Oxford Road, Reading, Berkshire

© *Copyright 1974 James Hewitt*
All rights reserved

ISBN 85045 161 2

Printed in England by C. Tinling & Co. Ltd,
London and Prescot

Preface

Resistance in Ireland to English domination might be said to have begun with Strongbow's invasion of 1170, two years after which Pope Adrian IV (an Englishman) granted England's King Henry II the right to govern Ireland. The position was further complicated by the Protestant Reformation and, through plantations, by the establishment of a Protestant Ascendancy in Ireland. The firmly-rooted Protestant plantation of Ulster dates from 1608, and the roots of the present conflict in Ireland's north stretch back over three centuries.

Irish resistance has been both constitutional and revolutionary. This book is concerned with the latter strand, always simmering and periodically erupting in armed conflict: in the great rebellion of 1641, ruthlessly crushed by Cromwell, in the support for James II in 1689-90, in the bloody revolt of 1798, in the minor outbreaks of 1803, 1848, and 1867, and in the fascinating and romantic rising of Easter Week 1916, leading to the independence of twenty-six counties of Ireland and the stubborn loyalty to the British Crown of the Protestant majority in the remaining six.

The eye-witness material in this book is drawn from rebel and loyalist, Catholic and Protestant, people hotly committed or helplessly caught up in the current of violence. Availability – those who rebelled and lost were less likely than the winners to rush into print – and quality determined the compiler's choice, and accounts for any imbalance between opposing forces that might occur in any section. Consider, too, the potential wealth of recorded reminiscence that was snuffed out with the lives of executed rebel leaders: in particular, one thinks of the writers and poets among the shot leaders of Easter Week 1916. But if seventeenth century material tends to weigh more heavily on the pro-English side, the balance is redressed in the subsequent revolts to the satisfaction of all but the line-counting partisan.

Though, inevitably, opinions and prejudices here and there obtrude, the editor has sought out accounts from witnesses who reported sincerely what they saw, heard, and felt – many of them compassionate people who, like James Connolly, were 'willing to say a prayer for all honest men who do their duty'. In some cases in journals or diaries written within minutes and hours of what is described, we have accounts of historical events that have been transmogrified into the folklore of Orange and Green.

In common with other works in this series, this book is offered as a complement to the reading of conventional histories. Brian Inglis's *The Story of Ireland* makes a good introduction, or Professor J. C. Beckett's *A Short History of Ireland*, which is lucid and objective. Robert Kee's *The Green Flag* is a detailed study of Irish nationalism, and shatters a few popular myths. Thomas Pakenham's *The Year of Liberty* is a highly readable account of the great rebellion of 1798 that draws on a wealth of source material. Cecil Woodham Smith's *The Great Hunger*, though about the potato famine, has a sizable account of the Young Irelanders' rising of 1848, which can receive only brief mention herein. The standard work on the 1916 rising is Max Caulfield's *The Easter Rebellion*.

JAMES HEWITT

Contents

Preface	v
Acknowledgments	viii
List of Illustrations	ix
Chronicle of Events in Irish History	xi
Map of Ireland	xiv
The Great Rebellion: 1641–52	1
James versus William: 1688–91	33
The Rebellion of 1798	55
Three Minor Risings: 1803 – 1848 – 1867	111
Easter Week 1916	121
Sources	166
Index	171

Acknowledgments

Thanks are due to J. W. Vitty, Librarian of the Linen Hall Library, Belfast, for locating and supplying the editor with material concerning the rebellions in County Antrim and County Down in 1798.

Thanks are also due to the following for permission to reproduce the illustrations appearing in this book: City Museum and Art Gallery, Birmingham, for Plate 1; the Northern Ireland Tourist Board for Plate 2; the Ulster Museum, Belfast, for Plates 3, 4, 6, 7, 8 and 17; the National Library of Ireland for Plates 5, 11, 12, 13, 14 and 18; the Public Record Office of Northern Ireland for Plates 15 and 16; the Mansell Collection for Plates 19, 20, 21, 22 and 24; Syndication International for Plates 23, 25 and 26; the President of the Republic of Ireland and the National Gallery of Ireland for Plate 9; and the Library of Trinity College, Dublin, for Plate 10.

In some cases it has proved impossible to identify ownership, and apologies are extended for consequent failure to obtain permission for reproduction.

Illustrations

PLATES

1. Portrait of Oliver Cromwell by Lely
2. William of Orange, the Protestant hero, receives idealized depiction on banners carried in traditional Orange parades in Northern Ireland.
3. The death of Schomberg
4. Wolfe Tone
5. Suspected rebels being subjected to torture by pitch-capping
6. Henry Joy McCracken
7. Henry Joy McCracken's National Volunteer uniform
8. James Hope
9. The Battle of Ballynahinch
10. Death mask of Wolfe Tone
11. Robert Emmet
12. William Smith O'Brien
13. Thomas Francis Meagher
14. Charles Gavan Duffy
15. March past in Belfast of the 36th (Ulster) Division, May 1915

List of Illustrations

16 General Sir George Richardson and Sir Edward Carson
17 Ulster's Solemn League and Covenant
18 Proclamation of the Republic
19 James Connolly
20 A British machine gun section in the South Dublin area, April 1916
21 Rebels take position behind a barricade, Dublin 1916
22 The burned out G.P.O. in Dublin
23 Rebel prisoners being marched out of Dublin, May 1916
24 Count Plunkett's three sons – Joseph, George, and John, after surrender
25 Britain's Irish problem persists. Troops face I.R.A. bombers and snipers in Belfast 1969
26 The blazing British Embassy in Dublin, 2 February 1972

Chronicle of Events in Irish History

432 St. Patrick begins mission in Ireland
795 First Danish raids
1014 Brian Boru defeats the Danes at Clontarf
1170 Strongbow's invasion
1171 Henry II lands
1172 Pope Adrian IV 'grants' to Henry II right to govern Ireland
1315 Edward Bruce invades
1367 The Statutes of Kilkenny
1534 Rebellion of Silken Thomas
1536 Henry VIII extends the Act of Supremacy to Ireland
1541 Henry VIII takes the title King of Ireland
1559 Rebellion of Shane O'Neill
1569 First Fitzgeralds of Desmond revolt
1579 Second Desmond revolt
1586 Plantation of Munster
1598 Victory of Hugh O'Neill at the Yellow Ford
1601 Spanish land and are defeated at Kinsale
1603 Revolts finally suppressed by Mountjoy
1607 'Flight of the Earls' marking end of the Gaelic era
1608 Plantation of Ulster
1641 Rebellion on large scale. Massacre of Protestants and reprisals
1642 The Catholic Confederation founded
1645 Rinuccini, Papal Nuncio, arrives
1646 Owen Roe O'Neill wins Battle of Benburb

Chronicle of Events in Irish History

1649   Rinuccini leaves. Owen Roe O'Neill dies. Cromwell lands, storms Drogheda and Wexford
1652   Rebellion finally supressed. The Cromwellian Settlement
1660   Restoration of Charles II
1685   Accession of James II
1689   Siege and relief of Derry
1690   William defeats James at Battle of Boyne
1691   The Treaty of Limerick
1695   First of the penal laws
1778   Irish Volunteers formed
1783   Legislative autonomy for Ireland
1791   Society of United Irishmen founded
1796   Storm prevents French landing
1798   Rising on wide scale in May. French land in August. Rebellion crushed
1800   Parliamentary Union of Great Britain and Ireland
1803   Robert Emmet's rebellion. Emmet executed
1828   Daniel O'Connell elected M.P. for County Clare
1829   O'Connell takes seat. Catholic Emancipation
1840   Repeal Association founded by O'Connell
1845   Potato crop fails. The Great Famine 1845-1850
1848   Smith O'Brien's rebellion
1849   James Fintan Lalor's rising
1858   The Irish Republican Brotherhood founded in America
1867   The Fenian Rising
1871   The Church of Ireland disestablished
1875   Charles Stewart Parnell enters parliament
1879   The Land League founded
1881   Gladstone's Land Act
1882   The Phoenix Park murders
1886   Gladstone's First Home Rule Bill defeated
1890   Divorce Court verdict against Parnell. Deposed from leadership of the Irish Parliamentary Party
1891   Death of Parnell
1893   Gladstone's Second Home Rule Bill passed by Commons, rejected by Lords

1912 471,000 Ulster Protestants sign anti-Home Rule Covenant. Third Home Rule Bill
1913. Ulster Volunteer Force and Irish National Volunteers formed
1914 The Curragh Mutiny. U.V.F. land German guns at Larne, I.N.V. at Howth. First World War
1916 Easter Week Rebellion. Leaders executed
1917 Irish political prisoners (including Eamon de Valera) released
1919 Dail Eireann founded. Irish Government set up
1920 Warfare between the I.R.A. and British forces
1921 Treaty signed between Great Britain and Ireland. Irish Free State set up. Six north-eastern counties remain in the United Kingdom
1922–1923 Civil War between Free State and Republican forces
1939–1945 Second World War. Irish neutrality in the twenty-six counties
1949 Ireland finally becomes an independent republic. Commons in London passes the Ireland Act. Special status for Irish nationals in Great Britain; Northern Ireland to remain part of U.K. unless the people vote otherwise
1968 Civil Rights Movement founded in Northern Ireland
1969–1973 I.R.A. campaign of bombings and attacks on police and military. Sectarian clashes and assassinations
1972 British Government prorogues parliament of Northern Ireland
1973 Elections for new power-sharing Assembly in Northern Ireland. Referendum majority in Northern Ireland for remaining part of the United Kingdom

The Great Rebellion

1641-1652

'*Pro Deo, Pro Rege, Pro Hibernia Unanimis*' – 'One for God, King, and Ireland'.

    Slogan of the Irish Catholic Confederacy, founded 1642.

I had rather be overrun with a cavalierish interest than a Scotch interest; I had rather be overrun by a Scotch interest than an Irish interest, and I think of all this is most dangerous.

    Oliver Cromwell, to the Council of State, 15 March 1649.

It hath pleased God to bless our endeavours at Drogheda. The enemy were about three thousand strong in the town. . . . I believe we put to the sword the whole number of the defendants.

    Oliver Cromwell, letter dated 16 September 1649.

Whatever else may be said about Cromwell in Ireland (and plenty has), for historians he tied up a long period of unrest, complexity, and confusion. England's domination and colonization of Ireland had been irresolute and incomplete from the start, and subject to repeated rebellion: Cromwell applied resolution and brought settlement, for a time.

Modern Irish nationalism looks back to the Gaels as the 'first Irish', though there had been waves of Greek and Spanish invaders before the Gaels landed and won the struggle for the land and soul of Ireland less than a century before the conversion to Christianity. The first Danish raids were in 795. When High King Brian Boru (in some eyes the first Irish patriot) defeated the Danes at Clontarf in 1014, it was a fight between native factions, one with Norse support. An element of civil war, Irishman fighting Irishman, is invariably present in Irish wars and rebellions.

The roots of English domination begin in the twelfth century. Dermot MacMurrough, a defeated Irish King, asked for help from some Cambro-Norman barons, whose leader, the Earl of Pembroke, known as Strongbow, led a band of adventurers who captured Dublin and Waterford. Strongbow married Dermot's daughter (a condition of help) and became King of Leinster when MacMurrough died the in following year, 1171. The invaders were not Englishmen; they spoke Norman French; but they owed feudal allegiance to Henry II of England. Henry himself landed in Ireland in October 1171, staying until the following April. In return for Henry's entrenching papal power and collecting taxes for the Church, Pope Adrian IV, an Englishman, 'granted' Henry the right to govern Ireland. In effect it meant that Henry came to terms with the Irish chiefs, who were happy enough to recognize his feudal 'lordship of Ireland' as long as it did not interfere with their tribal rights. It should be understood that the Gaelic clan system could provide only a loose unity and that only the rudiments of Irish nationhood existed for several centuries.

The Anglo-Norman settlers established real control only in a small area along the coast in and near Dublin, which became known as the Pale. Beyond the Pale they intermarried with the Irish and adopted Irish customs. Many family names now looked upon as Irish to the core – Burke, Joyce, Fitzgerald, Costello, Prendergast, for example – were in fact Norman: de Burgo = Burke, de Jorz = Joyce, and so on. But where, mostly within the Pale, the identity of settlers from England remained clear-cut, they came to be known as Old English.

The English colonization of Ireland was never harmonious and the conquest always incomplete. Law and order was never established in fullness. Sectional interests were structured early. The Anglo-Irish, or Old English, class developed their own interests, and became a distinct group that was different from both native Irish and the English in England. The Reformation complicated matters further by adding religious divisions and tensions.

Edward Bruce brought over a Scottish force and enlisted Irish support in fighting the English, but was defeated in 1318.

The Statutes of Kilkenny, passed in 1366, were designed to stop the English settlers from being absorbed by the Irish. They forbade intermarriage between settlers and natives, and the speaking of the Irish language. They remained in force for two centuries, but were never fully effective. The statutes shaped the legal relations of English and Irish in Ireland until the reign of James I: the former came under English law, whereas the latter, under their chiefs, had their own Gaelic Brehon law. This further served to separate the two peoples. This was the position until Chichester's parliament (1613–15) declared the statutes null and void, and the Irish subjects of the British Crown. However, individual Irishmen were granted charters by the Viceroy bringing them under English law, and the Anglo-Irish lords made treaties with Irish chiefs that brought them under English law.

The rudiments of an Irish parliament took shape under Edward I (1272–1307) and was brought to fruition late in the reign of Edward III (1327–1377); but its rule, despite claims to embrace the whole of Ireland, was restricted chiefly to within the Pale. Richard II (1377–1399) on visiting Ireland made the distinction (in a letter to his uncle) between 'the wild Irish, our enemies; English rebels, and obedient English'.

The Irish, who repeatedly backed the losing side in disputes for the English throne, supported the pretender, Lambert Simnel, crowned King Edward VI of England and Ireland in Dublin in 1487.

In 1494 Henry VII sent Edward Poynings to Ireland with a small army and officials. The Pale, which had become increasingly independent, was brought under English authority: Poynings' Law saw to it 'that no parliament be holden in this land until the acts be certified into England'. Distance and the intervening sea made communication between London and Dublin difficult, so that the settlers in Ireland for several centuries were able to show a considerable measure of independence from the Crown. The Fitzgeralds were particularly powerful, until that power was broken by Henry VIII, who in 1541 had himself proclaimed in Dublin 'King of this land of Ireland as united, annexed and knit for ever to the Imperial Crown of the Realm of England'. Hitherto English monarchs had been content with the feudal 'lordship of Ireland'. Henry VIII was determined to break the power of both the Old English and the Gaelic chiefs. Gaelic Brehon law structured a system whereby the land was held by a tribe, ruled by a chief. Henry's 'surrender and regrant' offer enabled chiefs to surrender their lands and immediately receive them back as grants from the king. But whereas land had been held by a chief only for his lifetime, Henry's grant was based on inheritance by the eldest son.

Henry was able to make deals with the chiefs over land; but the souls of the people were not for sale: they looked to the counter-reformation papacy as the authority to which they owed their allegiance. To the Irish, Henry's rift with the papacy severed his right to govern Ireland.

The Reformation had been easily absorbed in England; in Ireland it made no headway at all. Apart from an unmistakable lack of will, there were several obstacles to conversion to Protestantism: 1. A ruthless attempt at conversion was not made. 2. The native Irish population was physically remote, and 3. intellectually remote through the barrier of the Gaelic language which they retained. 4. Henry's suppression of the monasteries, abbeys, and other institutions of the Church brought the Roman Catholic faith into the people's homes through wandering priests and friars. 5. The Old English were Catholic and the Crown wished to retain their loyalty, which might have been lost by pressing hard for conversion.

Henry VIII lived, and died, professing the Catholic faith, though Archbishop Cranmer and some of Henry's ministers were pushing the new Lutheran ideas. Mary (1553–1558) had Cranmer and hundreds of Protestants burned at the stake. Their martyrdom did much for the Protestant cause: even more the accession of Elizabeth (1558). Rome recognized Mary Queen of Scots as the rightful heir to the throne; Elizabeth passed an Act of Supremacy that placed herself at the head of the Church in England and made England Protestant. During her reign the Calvinists complained that the Church in England adhered too closely to Romish doctrine and needed purification. These Puritans, as they were called, were soon strong in parliament: in the next century they found an iron leader in Oliver Cromwell. Elizabeth survived a series of counter-reformation plots. In February 1570 Pope Pius V excommunicated her. The massacre of French Protestants on St Bartholomew's Day 1572 and the horrors of the Spanish Inquisition had the effect of making Protestants even more determined to hold on to their faith, in the same way that persecution more firmly entrenched Catholicism in the Irish.

Elizabeth overcame a series of rebellions in Ireland. With England Protestant, the rebels turned to Catholic powers on the continent for arms. James Fitzmaurice Fitzgerald organized a landing by a mixed force of Italians and Spaniards, financed by the Pope and the King of Spain. The outcome was that Elizabeth confiscated lands in Munster where the invaders had landed and resettled them with English Protestants. The most serious opposition for Elizabeth came from Ulster's Hugh O'Neill, who had been brought up at the English Court. He took the forbidden ancient title 'The O'Neill', and inflicted England's worst defeat at Irish hands at the Battle of Yellow Ford. Inspired by this success, other Gaelic chiefs rose against the settlers. The Munster plantations were undone. The rebellion was broken by Lord Mountjoy before four thousand Spaniards landed at Kinsale in 1601. They promptly surrendered and returned home. O'Neill, master of irregular warfare, fought on for a year before agreeing terms.

The submission of Hugh O'Neill in March 1603, six days after the *death of Queen Elizabeth I, marks the completion of the Tudor conquest. Professor Beckett (A Short History of Ireland) considers the main object of Tudor policy 'was to make sure that Ireland should not become a centre of intrigue for English rebels or continental enemies. Despite the fact that it issued in military conquest, Tudor policy in Ireland was essentially defensive.' The completion of the conquest brought the breaking up of Gaelic Ireland. The old Brehon laws were abolished and English law and administration extended throughout Ireland. Hitherto Irish chiefs had been allowed to have private armies; now only the royal army was permitted. Rather than join the army of the Crown, thousands of native Irish soldiers sailed to serve in the Catholic armies of France and Spain. There was a more serious emigration for the history of Ireland: O'Neill, Earl of Tyrone, O'Donnell, Earl of Tryconnel, and ninety-eight other Irish chiefs found an anglicized Ireland impossible to live in and went into exile on the continent. During Mary's reign what are now the counties of Leix and Offaly, whose chiefs had been rebellious, were planted with English settlers; but this was a minor affair compared with the plantations following the end of the Tudor conquest. 'The Flight of the Earls' left most of the land of Ulster available for settlement. The settlers were 150,000 Scottish Presbyterians and 20,000 English Protestants; their settlement was tenacious and permanent. The origins of the partitioning of Ireland in the twentieth century and the conflicts resulting from it have their origins in the plantation of Ulster that followed the 'Flight of the Earls'.*

In England the Puritan faction was becoming militant. James I relaxed many of the pressures against the Catholics, but he had to be careful not to upset the Protestants. The Gunpowder Plot destroyed any further chances of help for the Catholics from the king. Charles I inherited from his father, James I, a belief in the Divine Right of kings, and a quarrel with the parliamentary Puritans who believed in divine right neither for popes nor kings. Charles sent Sir Thomas Wentworth to Dublin as viceroy in 1633, with the mission of establishing a stabilized Ireland that would bolster the royal cause. The strong army he built up alarmed the parliamentarians; his strengthening of the position of the Protestant Established Church aroused fears in the Catholics. By 1641 there were several factions in Ireland whose interests clashed: the Old

English, Catholics, fearful of militant Puritanism; the New English, divided between loyalty to the king and the cause of the parliamentarians; the native Irish gentry and peasantry, in a rebellious mood; and the Ulster planters, mostly Scots and Dissenters, uncertain where their loyalties lay in the English dispute.

Out of this confused situation came the 1641 rebellion. Religion and land were the two exposed nerves that carried its current. Plans were laid for a widespread insurrection, stamped symbolically on the first day, 23 October, by the seizing of Dublin Castle. The plan for Dublin was betrayed, and the Castle was not taken; but the rebellion went ahead, starting in Ulster. The native Irish, including bands of men who, on losing their lands, had taken to a life of brigandage, slaughtered thousands of Protestant settlers – men, women, and children. There were counter-atrocities, equally horrible. On the night of 22 October Sir Phelim O'Neill seized Charlemont, on the main route north over the Blackwater River, and in many places in Ulster castles and forts were seized. On the 24th O'Neill issued a proclamation from Dungannon, which he had taken, disclaiming that the rebellion was directed against the king, but in defence of the liberties of the Irish people. By 4 November the rebels were in control of the counties of Armagh, Tyrone, Donegal, Fermanagh, Monaghan, Cavan, Leitrim, Longford, and part of Down.

The rebellion rapidly spread south to the counties around Dublin. Sir John Temple observed the plight of the Protestant refugees who poured into the city:

Thus was the town, within the compass of a few days after the breaking out of this rebellion, filled with those most lamentable spectacles of sorrow, which in great numbers wandered up and down in all parts of the city, desolate, forsaken, having no place to lay their heads on, no clothing to cover their nakedness, no food to fill their hungry bellies. And to add to their miseries, they found all manner of relief very disproportionable to their wants, the Popish inhabitants refusing to administer the least comfort onto them; so as those sad creatures appeared like living ghosts in every street. Many empty houses in the city, where by special direction taken up for them: barns, stables, and out-houses filled with them, yet many lay in the open streets, and others under stalls, and there most miserably perished. The churches were the common receptacles of the meaner sort of them, who stood there in most doleful posture, as objects of charity, in so great multitudes, that there was scarce any passage into them. But those of better quality, who could not frame themselves to be common beggars, crept into private places; and some of them, that had not private friends to relieve them, even walked silently away, and so died without noise. And so bitter was the remembrance of their former condition, and so insupportable the burden of their present calamity to many of them, as they often refused to be comforted. I have known of some that lay almost naked, and having clothes sent, laid them by, refusing to put them on. Others that would not stir to fetch themselves food, though they knew where it stood ready for them. But they continued to lie nastily in their filthy rags, and even their own dung, not taken care to have any thing clean, handsome or comfortable about them. And so even worn out with the misery of the journey and cruel usage, having their spirits spent, their bodies wasted, and their senses failing, lay here pitifully languishing; and soon after they had recovered this town, very many of them died, leaving their bodies as monuments of the most inhuman cruelties used towards them. The greatest part of the women and children thus barbarously expelled out of their habitations, perished in the city of Dublin: and so great numbers of them were brought to their graves, as all the churchyards within the whole town were of too narrow a compass to contain them.[49]

A rebel oath of association used circa *November 1641 indicates that this was not a rebellion against the Crown.*

... to maintain and defend, as far as I may, with my life, power and estate, the public and free exercise of the true and Catholic Roman religion against all persons that shall oppose the same: I further swear that I will bear faith and allegiance to our sovereign lord King Charles, his heirs and successors, and that I will defend him and them, as far as I may, with my life, power, and estate, against all such persons as shall attempt anything against their royal persons, honours and estates or dignities, and against all such as shall directly or indirectly endeavour to suppress their royal prerogatives, or do any act or acts contrary to regal government, as also the power and privileges of parliament, the lawful rights and privileges of the subjects, and every person that makes this vow, oath and protestation. . . .[36]

One of the minor incidents typical of the rebellion in its early stages was described in the journal of Maurice Cuffe, who defended the Castle of Ballyally, besieged by rebels from 1 November 1641 to 15 June 1642. Later in 1642 the castle fell to Lt-Col. Christopher O'Brien, created Baron of Inchiquin by the Supreme Council of Kilkenny. For period flavour, the original spelling has been retained. The extract gives us a glimpse of some of the more eccentric military tactics of the time, including an Irish version of the Trojan Horse – the Great Sow.

The great sow was 35 foote long and 9 foote broade; it was made upon 4 wheeles mad of whole timbar, bound aboutt with hoopes of iron, there axell trees where one she run was great round bars of iron, the beames she was bult upon being of timbar. Thaie had cros beames within to worck with there levars, to forse har along as thaie plesed to gide har. The hindar part of the sow was left open for there men to go in and outt at. The fore parte of the sow had 4 dowres, 2 in the ruffe and 2 one of the lowar parte, which did hang upon great iron huckes, but were not to open tell thaye came close to the wale of the castell, where thaie intended to worck through the castell with there tooles thaie had provided. The ruffe of the sow was bult lick the ruffe of a howse, with a very sharp ridge; the lowar parte as the wales of a howse. She was dubell plancked with manie thik oken planckes, and driven very thick with 5 stroke nailes, which nailes cost 5[11]. being intended for a howse of corection which should have bin bult at Inish. This sow was lickwaies covard with 2 rowes of hides and 2 rowes of sheepe skinnes, soe that noe musket bullet or steele arow could pearse it, of which triell was often made.[17]

There was, too, a lesser sow . . .

. . . being but 6 foote long and 3 foote brod, bult strong, as above, only run but upon one wheele lick a wheele barrow, and cheefely inployd to goe for vittell for the great sow to the camp, and for any to com to the bigg sow when thaie desired.[17]

The witness gives this description of a leathern piece of ordnance made by the castle's besiegers:

The said peece was about 5 foote in length, not bult upon caredge, but fastened in a stocke of timber. This goon thaie planted in the great trench, neere the castell, to be redy when thaie found accation to discharge har, the dimetrie being aboutt 5 inches; the lethar thaie made har withall was leetell bettar then halfe tand. ... The next morning thaie made triell of there lethern gun at us, but shee only gaue a great report, having 3[li] of powthar in har, but lett fly backwarde the bullet remaining within.[17]

The Great Sow was no less a failure. Both it and its piglet were taken by the castle's defenders on 27 February.

One the Sondaie morning my brothars and the rest of the men resolued to ventar forth for wattar, which most desparatly thaye performed, furst ventaring upon the men that were gon into the haggard, leving men suffishent within the castell to kepe the enemy of from releving the sow or haggard, which company in the haggard lost there lives, only one that shwam over the lough. Having had good succes heere, thaie then fell upon the sowes, recovering both, and kiling and mortall wounding all the men that were therein, only Abraham Baker, whom thaie tuck prisnor ... .[17]

Massacre stories, often exaggerated, inflamed anti-Catholic feeling in England and accounted in great part for the severity of Cromwell and his Ironsides in 1649. The eight years' gap before crushing action was taken against the rebels was due to the growing quarrel between Crown and Parliament in England. Following the outbreak of the insurrection, Parliament suspected the king of collusion with rebel leaders and refused to grant the permission and money needed to raise a powerful force to go to Ireland. What troops there were in Ireland were placed under the command of James Butler, 12th Earl of Ormonde, a leading royalist. He secured Dublin, and would have taken the offensive against the rebels had he been granted reinforcements earlier; they did not arrive until the end of 1641. Moving out from Dublin, Ormonde was able to relieve Drogheda in March 1642. In April, with Parliament's approval, General Robert Munro was sent to Ulster with a Scottish force of 2,500 men.

In England, civil war broke out in August 1642. Shortly afterwards the Irish rebels set up a government at Kilkenny and thereto summoned a 'general assembly for the kingdom of Ireland'. It was dominated by the Old English gentry, who had hesitated for about six weeks before siding with the rebels. This alliance of Old English Catholics and native Irish Catholics marks the first step in the development of Irish nationalism in its sectarian form. Hitherto the Old English had remained separatist, independent, and determined in safeguarding and expanding wherever possible their interest as a group. Their alliance with the native Irish was far from wholehearted. Their hesitation was understandable: by rebelling, the Old English risked losing much in land, property, and political influence. In 1641 Catholics still held two-thirds of cultivable land in Ireland.

The Kilkenny Assembly was convened in the autumn of 1642. It had an upper house whose members were bishops, abbots, and Catholic gentry, and a lower house consisting of members representing counties and boroughs. The Earl of Castlehaven attended the Assembly and was elected to the Supreme Council.

On my arrival at Kilkenny, I found the town very full, and many of my acquaintance, all preparing for war. To this end they had chosen amongst themselves, out of the most eminent persons, a Council, to which they gave the title of The Supreme Council of the Confederate Catholics of Ireland, and formed an oath of association, by which all were bound to obey them. They had made four generals for the respective provinces of the kingdom; Preston, of Leinster; Barry, of Munster; Owen Roe O'Neill, of Ulster; and one Bourke, of Connaught; and being to give commissions they caused a seal to be made, which they called the Seal of the Council. . . .

The first assembly met the 24th of October, 1642. It differed little from a Parliament, but that the Lords and Commons sat together. They approved, without delay, all the Council had done, and settled a model of government, viz:– That at the end of every general assembly, the Supreme Council should be confirmed or changed, as they thought fit. That it should consist of twenty-five, six out of each province, three of the six still resident; the 25th was myself, with no relation to any province, but to the Kingdom in general. Every province had a provincial assembly, which met on occasions; and each county had commissioners for applotting money within themselves, as it came to their shares, on the general applotment of the province. Many other things there were as to government, but these are the most remarkable.[5]

The Earl of Castlehaven considered that six main grievances were responsible for the Catholics rebelling.

First, they observed, that by the governors of that kingdom they were generally looked upon as a conquered nation, seldom or never treated like natural or free-born subjects: and for their further excuse, said besides, that a discontented people, while thus used, are very apt to think they are no longer obliged, then they are forced, to obedience; but may, by the same way they had lost, when able, regain their liberty.

Secondly, it grieved them extremely, that on the account of Tyrone's rebellion, as they said, six whole counties in Ulster were in a lump escheated to the crown, and little or nothing restored to the natives, though several of them never joined with Tyrone, but a great part bestowed by King James on his countrymen.

Thirdly, it did not a little heighten their discontent, that in the Earl of Strafford's time, there was a great noise of initiating the crown to the counties of Roscommon, Mayo, Galway, and Cork, with some parts of Tipperary, Limerick, Wicklow and others: And, they averred, and experience tells us, where the people's property is like to be invaded, neither religion nor loyalty is able to keep them within bounds, if they find themselves in a condition to make any considerable opposition. . . .

Fourthly, they found that since the sitting of this parliament, great severities were used against the Roman Catholics in England, and both Houses solicited by several petitions out of Ireland, to have those of that kingdom treated with the like rigour, which to a people so fond of their religion as the Irish, was no small inducement to make them, while there was an opportunity offered, to stand upon their guard.

Fifthly, they saw the Scots by pretending grievance, and taking up arms to get them redressed, had not only gained divers privileges and immunities, but got 300,000L. for their visit, besides 850L. a day for several months together. And this precedent encouraged the

Irish so much at that time, that they offered it to Owen O'Conelly who discovered their design as chief motive in rising then in rebellion; which, said he, 'They engaged in, to be rid of the tyrannical government that was over them, and to imitate Scotland, who by that course had enlarged their privileges.'

Lastly, they foresaw the storm draw on, and such misunderstandings daily arise between the king and parliament, as portended no less than a sudden rupture between them, which made these malcontents believe the king thus engaged, partly at home, and and partly with the Scotch, could not be able to suppress them so far off; and therefore, rather than hold out, would grant them any thing they could in reasoned demand, at least, more than otherwise they could expect.[5]

The aim of the Irish Catholic Confederacy was not independence, but a Catholic Ireland loyal to the Stuart Crown. Ireland as a separate nation was not the issue; Irish nationalism was a later growth. The confederation's slogan was 'Pro Deo, Pro Rege, Pro Hibernia Unanimis' or 'One for God, King, and Ireland.' The confederates were strong in numbers, but divided in leadership, both in council, where Old English and Irish mistrusted each other, and in the field. Owen Roe O'Neill, native Irish, a nephew of Hugh O'Neill who had so tormented Elizabeth, commanded in the North; Thomas Preston, from a leading Old English family of the Pale, led the rebel forces in Leinster. It seemed a fair distribution of military responsibility; but jealousy between them and a temperamental incompatability that took root when they served in the Spanish Netherlands, did not make for harmonious co-operation between the two commanders.

As England was caught up in a civil war lasting five years, the Protestants in Ireland were divided by the struggle, King versus Parliament. Ormonde and his army were loyal to Charles; but the Lords Justices and civil administrators in Dublin favoured the Parliamentarians. Charles instructed Ormonde to make a treaty with the Irish rebels, so that troops would be freed for the royal cause in England. In September 1643 Ormonde managed a cease-fire on behalf of his own force; but Munro and his Scots ignored it. Charles grew desperate and negotiated secretly with the rebels through the Earl of Glamorgan, a

Roman Catholic, who made a treaty which the king had publicly to repudiate when faced with an adverse reaction in England. The Irish and clerical faction in the Confederation pressed for confirmation of the treaty negotiated by the Earl of Glamorgan; the Old English faction had different ideas for a settlement.

A powerful figure joined the Confederation in Kilkenny in October 1645. Nuncio Giovanni Battista Rinuccini sailed to Ireland from Italy accompanied by a frigate carrying arms. He here describes his arrival and reception:

My first lodging was in a shepherd's hut in which animals also took shelter, and there I remained two days not so much to repose after our trials as to return thanks for our safety. The Secretary of the Confederation and others regretted much that we had not been able to land at Waterford, where, they said, I should have been received with prepared demonstrations, and firing of cannon. I, however, rejoiced greatly that fortune had brought me to a sterile and unknown part of the country where no Apostolic minister had ever been before... Having landed in Munster not very far from Cork, which is now in the hands of the Parliamentarians, every day brought new accounts of vessels stationed on the coast to take me, and it was reasonable to think that similar attempts would be made by land. I therefore travelled with great circumspection, often times leaving the high roads, posting sentinels about at night, sending spies on before, and taking in fact all the precautions necessary in war.... It would be impossible to give your Eminence [*letter was to Cardinal Pamphili*] an idea of the ruggedness of the roads, and the steepness of the mountains and passes over which this escort conveyed us and our baggage. My mind was not completely at ease until we had left the hostile country behind us... Of the arms which I brought from Paris I had a part landed and deposited in the castle of Ardtully, a strong post and approved of in the public name by Secretary Belling; the rest remained in the frigate. I had given orders that the vessel should go round to Waterford... The evening before my arrival at Kilkenny I stopped at a villa three miles from the town, to give time for all the preparations for my reception. Here I was visited by four noblemen on the part of the Council, accompanied by Mr Belling, who came to welcome me again, and one of them, a man of letters, pronounced a short oration. As soon as I was in my litter we set out, and in the space of those three miles I was met by all the nobility and by all the young men of Kilkenny, besides crowds of other persons in different detachments, the leaders of each dismounting to compliment me. The first to come was a band of fifty scholars, all however armed with pistols, who after caracoling round me conveyed their compliments to me through one of their number, a youth crowned with laurel and in a richer habit than the rest, and who recited some verses to me. . . . [41]

The Old English were still the stronger party in the confederation, and in March 1646, behind Rinuccini's back, they secured a new treaty with Ormonde. But before the treaty could be operated, Owen Roe O'Neill defeated Munro at Benburb, near Armagh, 5 June, a victory which tilted the balance of power in the Confederation towards the Pope's ambassador. There is a contemporary account of the battle thought to be by Captain Mulholland, a British officer serving with the regiment of Sir John Clotworthy. Owen Roe O'Neill is referred to throughout as McArt.

This year a Nuncio came from the Pope, and brought with him − of gold, and had them stamped to pistols and half pistols. At whose coming the Confederate Council of Kilkenny were consulting who to send to keep the Scots of Ulster from advancing through their country; and then considering with themselves how the Lord Castlehaven lost many of his army, and did nothing but stole away from the Scottish at last, they resolved to employ McArt [*Owen Roe O'Neill*], and so styled him Captain General of the Catholic Army of Ulster, with permission to raise seven regiments [of foot], and seven troops of horse − which accordingly he did. With some of these regiments were 1,500, as in his own and Colonel McDonall's, and in all the rest about 1,000 each.

After he raised these forces, he got arms for them, half muskets, half pikes, so he would have it, and pistols for four troops and lances for one. Then he marched from his winter quarters in March, and marched to a hill in the county of Cavan, called the Gallanagh, where he remained seven weeks training and exercising his men daily, and gave them sixpence per diem of the Pope's gold, so that hill is ever since called Cnock a-norr [*Cnoc an óir*] in Irish, the Hill of Gold.

Towards the end of seven weeks he got intelligence from Charlemont, that the British and Scottish Army were to rendezvous at a place called Benburb, within two miles of Charlemont, on the fifth of June; on which he marched towards it, discharging all the creates [or cattle-drovers] and ordered them all to return home; and came in the evening before the day to Benburb, ...

McArt made not his way to Charlemont but towards his enemies, and marched a mile from Benburb towards them, where he took his ground on a scroggred high hill, but sent out five hundred men more, half pike, half musket, to assist those returning from the Lord of Ardes, on which Ardes halted till Munroe came up with the army, and drew on another hill against McArt, and a bottom between them. Then men were commanded out from both sides down next the river in scroggie woods, where Munroe's men were often put to the worse and beaten back, and then [the parties were] relieved on both sides.

In the meantime that these parties or wings were so plain, Munroe's field pieces were not idle, but giving fire, and most commonly overshot McArt's men, [and] only twice struck down two files. At this rate they were from two o'clock till an hour before sunset, and McArt's men trying to advance. But he desired them to have a little patience till the horse would return, who returning in great haste at gallop, all in a sweat, both horse and men, and drawn up in their ground; then there was an intermission on both sides, being preparing to fight more close, on which McArt spoke in the front of his own men these words, as I was told, or to that effect:—

'Gentlemen and fellow soldiers! Know that those that stand before you ready to fight are those that banished you, your wives and children from your lands and houses, and make you seek your bread and livelihood in strange places. Now you have arms in your hands as good as they have, and you are gentlemen as good as they are. You are the flower of new Ulster, descended from as ancient and honourable stock of people as any in Europe. This land and your predecessors having possessed about three thousand years. All

Christendom knows your quarrel is good – to fight for your native birthright and for the religion which your foregathers professed and maintained since Christianity came first to this land.

So now is the time to consider your distressed and slavish condition; you have arms in your hands, you are as numerous as they are; and now try your valour and your strength on those who have banished you, and now resolve to destroy you bud and branch. So let your manhood be seen by your push of pike; and I will engage, if you do so, by God's assistance and the intercession of His Blessed Mother and all the Holy Saints in Heaven, that the day will be your own. Your word is *Sancta Maria*; and so in the name of the Father, of the Son, and of the Holy Ghost, advance, and give not fire till you are within pike-length.'

Which accordingly was observed. At which time sun and wind was against them, and blew the smoke in their faces, so that for a little moment the musketeers could not see. At which charge the Scottish and British officers stood it manfully, and left not their ground till they were beaten down by push of pike. But their men did not back them so vigorously as they should. One reason was, that since they left Mullow and Lisnegarvy they had not time to rest or refresh themselves till they came to front McArt, and then standing from two o'clock till seven o'clock to their arms, was enough to make them faint and heartless.

Another reason is that the Irish pikes were longer by a foot or two than the Scottish pikes, and far better to pierce, being four square and small, and the others' pikes, broad-headed, which are the worst in the world. Withall to my own knowledge, the soldiers, I mean some that were not strong [enough] in the British army for his pike on a windy day, would cut off a foot, and some two, of their pikes – which is a damned thing to be suffered. But the truth is, that army did not expect to be faced by Ulstermen, much less to be fought with; but too much confidence makes security, and security makes carelessness: and so it happened that day. . . .

The number killed there was about eighteen or nineteen hundred, besides one hundred and fifty odd taken prisoners, of private soldiers, whom McArt sent away with a convoy to Sir Charles Poines' pass with safety. The officers [who] got quarters, he sent to Charlemont....³⁴

The Irish victory at Benburb swung the balance of power at Kilkenny to the side of the clerical and native Irish party. Rinuccini was able to overthrow the Supreme Council, which had been dominated by the Old English faction, secure control for himself, and reject the treaty made with Ormonde. An attack was planned against Dublin by Preston and O'Neill, which their incompatability aborted. Ormonde faced surrender, and with the royalist cause in England sliding to defeat, he had to decide whether to surrender his forces to Irish or to English rebels: he chose the latter: there was always the possibility that Charles might patch up his quarrel with the Parliamentarians. On 18 June 1647 he handed over the forces and garrisons he controlled to a Parliamentary commander, and sailed to England. When Charles's cause showed signs of recovering, Ormonde returned to Ireland and set about organizing a royalist-confederate alliance. O'Neill, who had tried to make a deal with the Parliamentary commanders, offered support to Ormonde. Charles I was beheaded in London on 30 January 1649. In February Rinuccini left Ireland and returned to Italy.

Royalists now gave their allegiance to Charles's son, Prince Charles, then in Holland. With Charles's friend, Ormonde, in control of most of Ireland, though not Dublin or Londonderry, Cromwell decided it was time for the threat from Ireland to be crushed. On 15 March 1649, the Council of State, acting with the authority of Parliament, named Cromwell Commander-in-Chief of the army that would go to Ireland. He addressed the Council of Officers:

Truly this is really believed: if we do not endeavour to make good our interest there, and that timely, we shall not only have ... our interest rooted out there, but they will in a **very** short time be able to land forces in England and to put us to trouble here: and I confess I have had these thoughts with myself that perhaps may be carnal and foolish; I had rather be overrun with a cavalierish interest than a Scotch interest; I had rather be overrun by a Scotch interest than and Irish interest, and I think of all this most dangerous...¹⁶

Cromwell took the New Model Army to Ireland in August 1649: he stayed nine months, and, despite an illness, made victory certain before leaving Ireton (*his son-in-law*) and Ludlow to complete the conquest. Cromwell's letters to members of the Council of State in London provide the most gripping contemporary account of his campaign. He marched his army north from Dublin on *1* September and by the *3*rd he had about ten thousand men before Drogheda. They stormed the town on the evening of the *11*th.

Cromwell's letter to the Hon. John Bradshaw, President of the Council of State, has been quoted often:

It hath pleased God to bless our endeavours at Drogheds. After battery, we stormed it. The enemy were about three thousand strong in the town. They made a stout resistance; and near one thousand of our men being entered, the enemy forced them out again. But God giving a new courage to our men, they attempted again, and entered, beating the enemy from their defences. The enemy had made three entrenchments, both to the right and left 'of' where we entered; all of which they were forced to quit. Being thus entered, we refused them quarter; having, the day before, summoned the town. I believe we put to the sword the whole number of the defendants. I do not think thirty of the whole number escaped with their lives. Those that did, are in safe custody for the Barbadoes. Since that time, the enemy quitted to us Trim and Dundalk. In Trim they were in such haste that they left their guns behind them.

This hath been a marvellous great mercy. The enemy, being not willing to put an issue upon a field-battle, had put into this garrison almost all their prime soldiers, being about three thousand horse and foot, under the command of their best officers; Sir Arthur Ashton being made governor. There were some seven or eight regiments, Ormond's being one, under the command of Sir Edmund Verney. I do not believe, neither do I hear, that any officer escaped with his life, save only one lieutenant, who, I hear, going to the enemy said, that he was the only man that escaped of all the garrison. Upon this the enemy were filled with much terror. And truly I believe this bitterness will save much effusion of blood, through the goodness of God. I wish that all honest hearts may give the glory of this to God alone, to whom indeed the praise of this mercy belongs....[15]

The Great Rebellion: 1641-52

A more detailed account of the storming of Drogheda was written by Cromwell for the Hon. William Lenthall, Speaker of the Parliament of England:

Your army being safely arrived at Dublin; and the enemy endeavouring to draw all his forces together about Trim and Tecroghan, as my intelligence gave me, – from whence endeavours were made by the Marquis of Ormond to draw Owen Roe O'Neill with his forces to his assistance, but with what success I cannot yet learn, – I resolved, after some refreshment taken for our weather-beaten men and horses, and accommodations for a march, to take the field. And accordingly, upon Friday the 30th of August [*actually 31st*] last, rendezvoused with eight regiments of foot, six of horse and some troops of dragoons, three miles on the north side of Dublin. The design was, To endeavour the regaining of Tredagh; or tempting the enemy, upon his hazard of the loss of that place, to fight.

Your army came before the town upon Monday following. Where having pitched, as speedy course was taken as could be to frame our batteries; which took up the more time because divers of the battering guns were on shipboard. Upon Monday the 9th [*10th*] of this instant, the batteries began to play. Whereupon I sent Sir Arthur Ashton, the then Governor, a summons, To deliver the town to the use of the Parliament of England. To the which receiving no satisfactory answer, I proceeded that day to beat down the steeple of the church on the south side of the town, and to beat down a tower not far from the same place, which you will discern by the chart enclosed.

Our guns not being able to do much that day, it was resolved to endeavour to do our utmost the next day to make breaches assaultable, and by the help of God to storm them. The place pitched upon was that part of the town wall next a church called St Mary's; which was the rather chosen because we did hope that if we did enter and possess that church, we should be the better able to keep it against their horse and foot until we could make way for the entrance of our horse; and we did not conceive that any part of the town would afford the like advantage for that purpose with this. The batteries planted were two: one was for that part of the wall against the east end of the said church; the other against the wall on the south side. Being somewhat long in battering, the enemy made six retrenchments: three of them from the said church to Duleek Gate; and three of them from the east end of the church to the town wall and so backward. The guns, after some two or three hundred shot, beat down the corner tower, and opened two reasonable good breaches in the east and south wall.

Upon Tuesday, the 10th [*11th*] of this instant, about five o'clock in the evening, we began the storm: and after some hot dispute we entered, about seven or eight hundred men; the enemy disputing it very stiffly with us. And indeed, through the advantages of the place, and the courage God was pleased to give the defenders, our men were forced to retreat quite out of the breach, not without some considerable loss; Colonel Castle being there shot in the head, whereof he presently died; and divers officers and soldiers doing their duty killed and wounded. There was a tenalia [*advanced defensive-work*] to flanker the south wall of the town, between Duleek Gate and the corner tower before mentioned; – which our men entered, wherein they found some forty or fifty of the enemy, which they put to the sword. And this tenalia they held: but it being without the wall, and the sally-port through the wall into that tenalia being choked up with some of the enemy which were killed in it, it proved of no use for an entrance into the town that way.

Although our men that stormed the breaches were forced to recoil, as is before expressed; yet, being encouraged to recover their loss, they made a second attempt: wherein God was pleased so to animate them that they got ground of the enemy, and by the goodness of God, forced him to quit his entrenchments. And after a very hot dispute, the enemy having both horse and foot, and we only foot, within the wall, – they gave ground, and our men became masters both of their retrenchments and 'of' the church; which, indeed, although they made our entrance the more difficult, yet they proved of excellent use to us; so that the enemy could not 'now' annoy us with their horse, but thereby we had advantage to make good the ground, that so we might let in our own horse; which accordingly was done, though with much difficulty.

Divers of the enemy retreated into the Mill-Mount: a place very strong and of difficult access; being exceedingly high, having a good graft, and strong pallisadoed. The Governor, Sir Arthur Ashton, and divers considerable officers being there, our men getting up to them, were ordered by me to put them all to the sword. And indeed, being in the heat of the action, I forbade them to spare any that were in arms in the town: and, I think, that night they put to the sword about 2,000 men; – divers of the officers and soldiers being fled over the bridge into the other parts of the town, where about 100 of them possessed St Peter's church-steeple, some the west gate, and others a strong round tower next the gate called St Sunday's. These being summoned to yield to mercy, refused. Whereupon I ordered the steeple of St Peter's Church to be fired, when one of them was heard to say in the midst of the flames: 'God damn me, God confound me; I burn, I burn.'

The next day, the other two towers were summoned; in one of which was about six or seven score; but they refused to yield themselves: and we knowing that hunger must compel them, set only good guards to secure them from running away until their stomachs were come down. From one of the said towers, notwithstanding their condition, they killed and wounded some of our men. When they submitted, their officers were knocked on the head; and every tenth man of the soldiers killed; and the rest shipped for the Barbadoes. The soldiers in the other tower were all spared, as to their lives only: and shipped likewise for the Barbadoes.

I am persuaded that this is a righteous judgment of God upon these barbarous wretches, who have imbrued their hands in so much innocent blood; and that it will tend to present the effusion of blood for the future. Which are the satisfactory grounds to such actions, which otherwise cannot but work remorse and regret. The officers and soldiers of this garrison were the flower of their army....[15]

Dr Nicholas Bernard, preacher at St Peter's, recounted how Colonel Hewson arrived at the church, saying ...

... he had orders to blow up the steeple (which stood between the choir and the body of the church), where about three score men were run up for refuge, but the three barrels of powder which he had caused to be put under it for that end, blew up only the body of the church . . .⁸

Later, that night . . .

. . . Hewson caused the seats of the church to be broken up, and made a great pile of them under the steeple, which, firing it, took the lofts wherein five great bells hung, and from thence it flamed up to the top, and so at once men and bells and roof came all down together, . . .⁸

Thomas Wood, brother of the Oxford historian, Anthony Wood, served with Cromwell's army in Ireland. His description (quoted by Anthony Wood) of children being used as shields and of women butchered at Drogheda is not confirmed from any other source; R. Bagwell (Ireland under the Stuarts) warns, 'The stories attributed to Thomas Wood, the great antiquary's brother, rest entirely on hearsay evidence, and Thomas was a noted buffoon.'

In 1650 . . . being often with his mother and brethren, he would tell them of the most terrible assaulting and storming of Tredagh [*Drogheda*], wherein he himself had been engaged. He told them that three thousand at least, besides some women and children, were, after the assailants had taken part, and afterwards all the town, put to the sword on the 11 and 12 Sept., 1649; at which time Sir Arthur Ashton, the governor, had his brains beat out and his body hacked and chop'd to pieces.

He told them, that when they were to make their way up to the lofts and galleries in the church and up to the tower where the enemy had fled, each of the assailants would take up a child and use it as a buckler of defence, when they ascended the steps, to keep themselves from being shot or brained. After they had killed all in the church, they went into the vaults underneath, where all the flower and choicest of the ladies had hid themselves. One of these, a most handsome virgin in a red and costly and gorgeous apparel, kneeled down to Thomas Wood with tears and prayers to save her life: and being struck with a profound pity, took her under his arm, went with her out of the church, with intention to put her over the works and let her shift for herself; but then a soldier perceiving his intentions, ran his sword . . . whereupon Mr Wood seeing her gasping, took away her money, jewels, etc., and flung her down over the works.[54]

Cromwell's ruthlessness at Drogheda is one of those events deeply scarred into the collective Irish national psyche, to be thrown in the faces of the English even today. But Maire and Conor Cruise O'Brien (A Concise History of Ireland) *make the cogent observation:* 'From a military point of view, the ferocity of Cromwell and his successors in Ireland, Ireton, and Ludlow, was not extraordinary by seventeenth-century standards. The action of Cromwell's which lingers in the folk memory – the sack of Drogheda – was hardly more ferocious or macabre than that of Cashel by Murrough O'Brien, Earl of Inchiquin, in 1646. One may suspect that the real shock administered by Cromwell came not so much from his cruelty as from his efficiency, and above all from the determined and systematic character of his anti-Catholicism.' *The vast majority of the persons put to the sword at Drogheda were either English or Old English soldiers of an English king, Cromwell's enemy in civil war; and the reason for the slaughter – that it would set an example that would save lives and shorten the campaign (the same reason given for the dropping of atomic bombs on Japan towards the close of the Second World War) – doubtless had that effect. What shocks most today is Cromwell's religious exultation at the killings.*

Religious fanaticism was as characteristic of the times as military savagery. Cromwell was a true Puritan, brought up to fear and hate Roman Catholicism. Moreover, the massacre of Protestants in the rebellion he was crushing had been publicized in England in a lurid and often exaggerated manner; Cromwell and his Ironsides were on a mission of retribution. The crusading element was not just on one side. The Elizabethan rebellions and the great rebellion of 1641 had crusading aspects that the historian cannot afford to ignore. When James Fitz-maurice landed from Spain at Dingle in July 1579, accompanied by friars and a bishop, he issued this proclamation: 'The cause of this war is God's glory, for it is our care to restore the outward rite of sacrifice and the visible honour of the holy altar which the heretics have impiously taken away.... We are on the side of the truth and they on the side of falsehood; we are Catholic Christians, and they are heretics...' *Friar O'Mellan, chaplain to Sir Phelim O'Neill, wrote a narrative of* the wars of *1641* in which he saw the deaths of heretics as the judgment of God. 'One religious fanaticism, that of England, engaged and overthrew the forces of another, that of Ireland,' says Patrick O'Farrell (Ireland's English Question). *'The English were to rid themselves quickly of what was to seem a brief crusading aberration: its legacy was not primarily religious, but in civil liberties. But Cromwell the Puritan had defeated the Irish Catholics, thus burning the cause of the counter-Reformation, the impress of religious division, deep into Irish soil.'* Mr O'Farrell adds: *'Ways and means aside, the Tudors lacked the conviction, the will, to impose their religious policy on Ireland. Conviction and will Cromwell had in abundance. He came too late, only to confirm a die already cast.'*

Following his success at Drogheda, Cromwell moved south, and by *3* October was calling on garrison commander, Colonel David Sinnott, to 'deliver the town of Wexford into my hands'. Sinnott sought 'honourable terms'. On the *11th* four representatives from the town brought out a list of 'propositions', to which Cromwell replied:

I have had the patience to peruse your Propositions; to which I might have returned an Answer with some disdain. But, to be short, – I shall give the soldiers and noncommissioned officers quarter for life, and leave to go to their several habitations, with their wearing-clothes; – they engaging themselves to live quietly there, and to take up arms no more against the Parliament of England. And the commissioned officers quarter for their lives, but to render themselves prisoners. And as for the inhabitants, I shall engage myself that no violence shall be offered to their goods, and that I shall protect the town from plunder.

I expect your positive answer instantly; and if you will upon these terms surrender and quit, 'and' shall, in one hour, send forth to me four officers of the quality of field-officers, and two aldermen, for the performance thereof, – I shall thereupon forbear all acts of hostility.

Yours servant,
OLIVER CROMWELL

Which 'Answer' indeed had no effect. For whilst I was preparing of it; studying to preserve the town from plunder, that it might be of the more use to you and your army, – the Captain [*of the castle*], who was one of the Commissioners, being fairly treated, yielded up the castle to us. Upon the top of which our men no sooner appeared, but the enemy quitted the walls of the town; which our men perceiving, ran violently upon the town with their ladders, and stormed it. And when they were come into the market-place, the enemy making a stiff resistance, our forces brake them; and then put all to the sword that came in their way. Two boatfuls of the enemy attempting to escape, being overprest with numbers, sank; whereby were drowned near three hundred of them. I believe, in all, there was lost of the enemy not many less then two-thousand; and I believe not twenty of yours from first to last of the siege. And indeed it hath, not without cause, been deeply set upon our hearts, that, we intending better to this place than so great a ruin, hoping the town might be of more use to you and your army, yet God would not have it so; but, by an unexpected providence, in His righteous justice, brought a just judgment upon them; causing *them* to become a prey to the soldier who in their piracies had made preys of so many families, and now with their bloods to answer the cruelties which they had exercised upon the lives of divers poor Protestants!...[15]

The British officer who earlier described the battle at Benburb now describes the storming of Clonmel by Cromwell's army:

Then Cromwell, hearing the Lord Lieutenant's forces [were] dispersed, took his opportunity of taking towns and castles without any great opposition, and sent two or three regiments of horse and foot before him to block up Clonmel at distance. Which was done about a month before himself appeared before it, who, soon as he came, drew close to it, and then sent his summons to Hugh Duff [Hugh Dubh O'Neill] to surrender it on good quarters and conditions.

To which answer was made, that he was of another resolution than to give up the town on quarters or conditions, till he was reduced to a lower station, and so wished him to do his best. On which Cromwell fell to his work, and planted his cannons, at which time and before several resolute sallies were made out, and sometimes with good success, and sometimes not. At this play they were like sons of Mars, till a long breach was made near one of the gates, but proved not level enough when night fell.

Within two hours after, the Major General sent out written two hundred men and officers with a good guide, through by-ways from a place of the wall next the river that was neglected by the besiegers, and fell on the backs of those in a fort not fully finished, behind them, and cut them all off before any relief came; on which immediately the next gate was opened before them, and [they] got in safe with the loss of half a dozen. The number killed in the fort was about sixty, being one of their companies.

After this Hugh Duff did set all men and maids to work, townsmen and soldiers, only those on duty attending the breach and the walls – to draw dunghills, mortar, stones, and timber, and made a long lane a man's height and about eighty yards length on both sides up from the breach, with a foot thick back at the back of it; and caused [to be] place[d] engines on both sides of the same, and two guns at the end of it invisible opposite to the breach, and so ordered all things against a storm.

Which [storm] was about eight o'clock in the morning in the month of January, and [the English] entered without any opposition; and but few [were] to be seen in the town till they so entered, that the lane was crammed full with horsemen, armed with helmets, back breast swords, musquetoons, and pistols. On which those in the front seeing themselves in a pound, and could not make their way further, cried out, 'Halt!' 'Halt!' on which those entering behind at the breach thought by those words, that all those of the garrison were running away, and cried out, 'Advance!' 'Advance!' as fast as those before cried, 'Halt!' 'Halt!' and so advanced till they thrust forwards those before them, till that pound or lane was full, and could hold no more.

Then suddenly rushes a resolute party of pikes and musqueteers to the breach, and scoured off and knocked back those entering. At which instance Hugh Duff's men within fell on those within the pound with shots, pikes, scythes, stones, and casting of great long pieces of timber with the engines amongst them; and then two guns firing at them from the end of the pound, slaughtering them by the middle or knees with chained bullets, that in less than an hour's time about a thousand men were killed in that pound, being atop one another.

At this time Cromwell was on horseback at the gate, with his guard, expecting the gates to be opened by those entered, till he saw those in the breach beaten back, and heard the cannons going off within. Then he fell off as much vexed as ever he was since he first put on a helmet against the king, for such a repulse he did not usually meet with.

The siege, at distance and close, being about five or six weeks, and by several sallies out and on the walls several of those within were lost, but many wounded and sick, at which the major general consulted with his officers, [and seeing] that their ammunition was gone, concluded to leave the town without Cromwell's leave, so at nightfall he imported the same to the mayor, one White, and advised him after he was gone about a dozen miles off as he might guess, to send privately out to Cromwell for licence to speak to him about conditions for the town; but not to make mention of himself on any account till he had done. After which advise to the mayor he marches away with his men about two hours after nightfall, and passed over the river undiscovered by a guard of horse that lay at the other side of the bridge, and [he] made no great halt till he reached a town called Ballynasack, twelve miles from Clonmel, where he refreshed his men, and then marched to Limerick.

Then the mayor, according as he was advised, about twelve o'clock at night sent out to Cromwell very privately for a conduct to wait upon His Excellency; which forthwith was sent to him, and an officer to conduct him from the wall to Cromwell's tent, who after some course compliments was not long capitulating, when he got good conditions for the town, such in a manner as they required.

After which Cromwell asked him if Hugh O'Neill knew of his coming out, to which he answered he did not, for that he was gone two hours after night fell with all his men, at which Cromwell stared and frowned at him, and said, 'You knave, have you served me so, and did not tell me so before.' To which the mayor replied, if His Excellency had demanded the question he would tell him. Then he asked him what that Duff O'Neill was; to which the mayor answered, that he was an over sea soldier born in Spain; on which Cromwell said, 'G- d-n you and your over sea!' and desired the mayor to give the paper back again. To which the other answered, that he hoped His Excellency would not break his conditions or take them from him, which was not the repute His Excellency had, but to perform whatsoever he had promised. On which Cromwell was somewhat calm, but said in a fury, 'By G- above he would follow that Hugh Duff O'Neill wheresoever so far he went.'

Then the mayor delivered the keys of the gates to Cromwell, who immediately commanded guards on them, and next morning himself entered, where he saw his men killed in the pound, notwithstanding which and his fury that Hugh Duff went off as he did, he kept his conditions with the town.[34]

After nine months in Ireland Cromwell returned to England confident that Ireland had been subdued: his son-in-law, Ireton, and Ludlow completed the mission. When the military conquest had ended, Cromwell imposed a settlement which he thought would solve England's Irish problem. Catholics and royalists were dispossessed of their lands, and given the choice of leaving the country or settling west of the Shannon – 'to Hell or Connaught'. The forfeited land was given to Cromwell's soldiers and supporters. About half the total land area of Ireland was replanted; and now, for the first time, most Irish land was owned by Protestants.

The Restoration brought hope to the dispossessed Old Catholics that they would regain their land; but Charles had to be careful not to perturb his Protestant subjects. Several hundred of Charles's supporters in Ireland were resettled on their lands, and restrictions on Catholics exercising their faith were eased – but most of the Cromwellian settlers remained. In 1641 Catholics held about three fifths of cultivable land in Ireland; by the end of the Restoration settlement they held about one fifth, and that mostly in infertile Connaught. But thousands of Catholics had stayed on their lands as tenants – the effect was to establish a new ruling class of Protestant landowning gentry, and a form of landlordism that was the cause of unrest in Ireland for more than two centuries.

The Catholic confederates had displayed a lamentable lack of unity; yet a rudimentary Catholic Irish nationalism had been born, and Cromwell, more than anyone, brought all Catholics together, by the severity with which he crushed the rebellion and applied his plantation policy afterwards. Before the century was out Catholics united in Ireland, – this time in a clear-cut polarization between them and the Protestants – yet again to back a king fighting for the throne of England. And again they backed a loser.

James versus William
1688-1691

When valiant Schomberg he was slain,
    King William thus accosted
His warlike men, for to march on,
    And he would be the foremost.
'Brave boys,' he said, 'be not dismayed
    For losing of one commander:
For God will be our king this day
    And I'll be general under.'

The Boyne Water.

'To the Glorious, Pious, and Immortal memory of the Great and Good King William, who freed us from Pope and Popery, Knavery and Slavery, Brass Money and Wooden Shoes, and he who refuses this toast may be damned, crammed and rammed down the Great Gun of Athlone.'

Orange toast on Irish glass goblet, Victoria and Albert Museum.

Irish Catholics had their expectations raised by the accession to the throne of England (1865) of James II, brother of Charles II, and a Catholic. They were not disappointed: James appointed a Catholic viceroy, Richard Talbot, Earl of Tyrconnell, and Catholics took positions in the administration, courts, and army. The Old English made a recovery to power and influence that frightened the Protestant settlers. James's attempts to further the interests of his co-religionists in England and Ireland aroused Protestant fears and opposition. His reign ended with his flight to France in 1688 and the Revolution Settlement of 1689. William, Prince of Orange, who had been successful with his Dutch army against the French, was invited to succeed James. Tyrconnell, who had raised a Catholic army in Ireland to serve James, held most of Ireland when James landed there on 12 March 1689. Protestants, fearing a repetition of the horrors of 1641, fled in thousands to England; those who stayed sought safety in strongholds like Enniskillen and Londonderry, which were besieged. Louis XIV provided James with French officers and troops, arms, ammunition, and money. An Irish Catholic Parliament was summoned and passed an act returning to Catholics all the land confiscated by Cromwell: but before the act could be enforced James was defeated by William.

Two events receive annual celebration from Orangemen. The first is the shutting of the gates of Londonderry in December 1688 by some apprentice boys in the face of a Catholic regiment and the subsequent siege lasting 105 days. The second is the victory of William over James at the Battle of the Boyne, fought 1 July 1690 (12 July, new style calendar). Something of the reality of both events can now be caught through the records of eye-witnesses.

The Rev. George Walker and George Holmes were within Londonderry during the siege by the army of King James, being appointed a governor and a captain respectively. They share the description of the *privations of the inhabitants and the lifting of the siege after provision ships got through to the city.*

The Rev. George Walker:

Being prevailed on to give an account of the siege of Londonderry, it is convenient, by way of preliminary, to take notice how that town came to be out of the hands of the Irish, when all places of the Kingdom of any strength or consideration were possessed by them. It pleased God so to infatuate the councils of my Lord Tyrconnell, that when the three thousand men were sent to England to assist his master against the invasion of the Prince of Orange, he took particular care to send away the whole regiment quartered in and about this city.

He soon saw his error, and endeavoured to repair it by commanding my Lord Antrim to quarter there with his regiment, consisting of a numerous swarm of Irish and Highlanders. Upon the 6th of December, they were upon their march in and about Newtown, (a market town belonging to Colonel George Philips, twelve miles distant from Derry). Colonel Philips having notice of this, and joining with it the apprehensions that they were under, of a general insurrection of the Irish intended on the 9th of December, and considering that Derry as well as other places was to be presently possessed by the Irish ... immediately dispatches a letter to Alderman Norman, giving an account of these matters and his opinion of them, and importuning him to consult with the sober people of the town and to set out the danger of admitting such guests among them. ...

Alderman Norman and the rest of the graver citizens were under great disorder and consternation, and knew not what to resolve upon. One of the companies was already in view of the town, and two of the officers within it, but the younger sort who are seldom so dilatory in their resolutions, got together, run in all haste to the main-guard, snatched up the keys, and immediately shut up all the four gates, and the magazine.[52]

George Holmes:

... on the 12th of April last the Irish army appeared before our city, but at that distance that one of our cannons had enough to do to reach them; but in short time they approached nearer to our walls. In the first first place we burned all our suburbs and hewed down all our brave orchards, making all about as plain as a bowling-green. About the 18th of April King James came within a mile of our walls, but had no better entertainment than bullets of 14, 16 and 22 pounds weight. He sent us a letter under his own hand, sealed with his own seal, to desire us to surrender, and we should have our own conditions. The messenger was a lord with a trumpet, and out of grand civility we sent three messengers, all gentlemen; but two of them ran away from us, and the other came again. In short, we would not yield.

Then we proceeded, and chose captains and completed regiments, made two governers. We had 116 companies in the city. All our officers fled away, so we made officers of those that did deserve to be officers. I was made captain. And then we began to sally out, and the first sally that we made we slew their French general and several of their men with the loss of nine or ten of our men, which was the the greatest loss that ever we lost in the field. Every day afterward we sallied out and daily killed our enemies, which put us in great heart; but it being so soon of the year, and we having no forage for our horses, we was forced to let them out, and the enemy got many. The rest of them died for hunger.

About the 20th of May the enemy gave us a general onset on all sides, but was so defeated that we were not troubled with them again for a week.... Ten days after that battle they came again very boldly, but in half an hour's time returned with greater loss than before. They began to run their approaches near us on one side. They came within 100 yards of us, and one night they attempted so near that one of them knocked at our gate and called for faggots to burn it with. This being in the dead of the night and our men being gone off their posts we were in some danger. The drums beat alarm, and we got a party together and sallied out at another gate, fell upon them and put them to the rout and recovered our own ground again, came so near them that we might have taken them alive, but we gave them old quarter. This night our great guns did execution with case-shot off the walls; that's musket bullets.

At this time they played abundance of bombs (the weight of many of them was near three hundredweight), which killed many people. One bomb slew seventeen persons. I was in the next room one night at my supper (which was but mean), and seven men were thrown out of the third room next to that we were in, all killed, and some of them in pieces. Into this city they played 596 bombs, which destroyed many of our people and demolished many of our houses. Cannon bullets flew as fast as you could count them, and as we took up their bullets we sent them back again post paid. Thus men, horses, and all went to destruction.

But at last our provision grew scant and our allowance small. One pound of oatmeal and one pound of tallow served a man a week; sometimes salt hides. It was as bad as Samaria, only we had no pigeon's dung. I saw 2s. a quarter given for a little dog, horse blood at 4d. per pint; all the starch was eaten . . . horse flesh was a rarity, and still we resolved to hold out.[27]

The Rev. George Walker:

July 27. – The garrison is reduced to 4456 men, and under the greatest extremity for want of provision, which does appear by this account taken by a gentleman in the garrison, of the price of food:

	L.	S.	D.
Horse flesh sold for, per pound		1.	8.
A quarter of a dog, (fattened by eating the bodies of the slain Irish)		5.	6.
A dog's head		2.	6.
A cat		4.	6.
A rat		1.	0.
A mouse			6.
A small flook taken in the river, not to be bought for money, or purchased under the rate of a quantity of meal			
A pound of greaves		1.	0.
A pound of tallow		4.	0.
A pound of salted hides		1.	0.
A quart of horse blood		1.	0.
A horse-pudding			6.

A handful of sea-wreck	.. ..	2.
A handful of chick-weed	.. ..	1.
A quart of meal, when found	.. ..	1. 0.

We were under so great necessity that we had nothing left unless we could prey upon one another: A certain fat gentleman conceived himself in the greatest danger, and fancying several of the garrison looked on him with a greedy eye, thought fit to hide himself for three days. Our drink was nothing but water, which we paid very dear for, and could not get without great danger; we mixed in it ginger and anniseeds, of which we had great plenty. Our necessity of eating the composition of tallow and starch, did not only nourish and support us, but was an infallible cure of the looseness; and recovered a great many that were strangely reduced by that distemper, and preserved others from it.[52]

Three days later Walker recorded in his journal the arrival of two provision ships in Londonderry, one of which had broken a boom set up across the Foyle. On the arrival of the provision ships the siege was lifted.

July 30. About an hour after sermon, being in the midst of our extremity, we saw some ships in the lough make towards us . . .

The *Mountjoy* of Derry, Captain Browning Commander, the *Phoenix* of Coleraine, Captain Douglas Master, being both loaden with provision, were convoyed by the *Dartmouth* frigate. The enemy fired most desperately upon them from the fort of Culmore, on both sides of the river; and they made sufficient returns, and with the greatest bravery. The *Mountjoy* made a little stop at the boom, occasioned by her rebound after striking and breaking it, so that she was run aground. Upon this the enemy set up the loudest huzzas, and the most dreadful to the besieged that ever we heard; fired all their guns upon her, and were preparing their boats to board her. Our trouble is not to be expressed at this dismal prospect, but by great Providence firing a broadside, the shock loosened her so that she got clear, and passed their boom.

Captain Douglas all this while was engaged, and the *Dartmouth* gave them very warm entertainment. At length the ships got to us to the unexpressible joy and transport of our distressed garrison, for we only reckoned upon two day's life, and had only nine lean horses left, and among us all one pint of meal to each man. Hunger and the fatigue of war had so prevailed among us, that of 7500 men regimented, we had now alive but about 4300, whereof at least one-fourth part were rendered unserviceable.[52]

The Rev. George Walker was killed at the Battle of the Boyne, fought a year and a day later.

George Holmes concludes:

Four days before we got relief from England we saw a great drove of cows very near us, and we were very weak, but we resolved to sally out, and in order thereto we played our great guns off the walls and sallied out on our enemy. I led the forlorn hope, which was about 100 men of the best we had, with which I ran full tilt into their trenches; and before our body came up we had slain 80 men, put many to the rout. We got arms enough and some beef, but durst not stay long, not above half an hour. This vexed our enemies much; they said we took them asleep. I praise God I had still my health, and has yet.

After the ships came in with provisions to us our enemies thought it was in vain to stay any longer, so on Lammas day they left us the wide fields to walk in. In the siege we had not above 60 men killed, except with the bombs killed. But I believe there died 15,000 men, women and children, many of which died for meat. But we had a great fever amongst us, and all the children died, almost whole families not one left alive. This is a true account of the siege of Londonderry.[27]

The defenders of Enniskillen were equally successful, surviving attacks led by the Duke of Berwick, James's illegitimate son, and Patrick Sarsfield, of Old English stock, who had served in the Life Guards during the reign of Charles II.

Following his success in England, William's army was engaged in securing Scotland; but he sent ten thousand troops under the aged Duke of Schomberg to begin the reconquest of Ireland. Schomberg's troops, from their arrival in mid-August, fared badly. In the autumn, fever killed so many of his men at their camp at Dundalk that Schomberg was forced to withdraw into Ulster. With three quarters of Ireland still held by the Jacobites, William decided he would raise a large army, take it to Ireland, and end the war there. He only got his way after threatening his bickering ministers that he would return to Holland and leave Queen Mary to govern in England. An army was prepared, made up of more than forty thousand seasoned troops of several nationalities. William personally supervised preparations: the army was well equipped with arms and ammunition, food, clothing, transport, and medical stores. Sir Christopher Wren designed a wooden hut for the king's use on the campaign. The army reached Ulster in May, and at various camps awaited William's arrival. After appointing a council of nine to assist Mary whilst he was in Ireland, William sailed and stepped on to Irish soil at Carrickfergus on 14 June 1690, and next day went on to Belfast. Bonfires announced the arrival of the king, who was eager to force a battle on the enemy. The French advised caution to James, but William's wish was granted.

William's army assembled and marched south on the 19th. The weather was exceptionally hot. A deserter brought in news that James's army was at Ardee, but when William reached Ardee on the 29th he discovered that James had crossed the Boyne the day before. On the 30th William marched six miles to camp in sight of the enemy, at a point where the ground sloped on both sides of the river. James had about 30,000 men; William 40,000.

A Danish force made up part of William's army of mixed nationalities. Christian V of Denmark received the following eye-witness account of the Battle of the Boyne from one of his subjects:

On the 29th of last month the king broke up the camp near Dundalk, and we proceeded that same day to Ardee, where, as had previously been resolved upon, we again pitched our tents. We were here informed that the enemy had taken up their position along the Boyne. At daybreak, on the 30th, we again broke up our camp. His Majesty caused the army to march in two columns, and placed himself at the head of the cavalry of the left wing. As we descended the small hills with which the northern part of this small kingdom is studded, we discovered a very fine plain watered by the Boyne. A few hours later we came in full sight of the enemy, encamped on the further side of the little river. On drawing nearer we perceived that, on the enemy's side, the bank was high and steep in several places. With the help of glasses it was discovered that the enemy had not suspected us to be so near, for the horses of the cavalry had been turned out to graze. The 'boutte-selle' was at once sounded, and we noticed some confusion in the camp. Meanwhile the king gave orders that the army should encamp on this side of the river, that it should be drawn up in two lines, and within range of the enemy. He then sent a part of his cavalry to line the bank. King James did the same on his side. He moreover caused a small battery to be thrown up, and its fire to be directed against our cavalry. This obliged the king to make it retire a little, as our artillery was not yet in the camp, and we could not return the fire. But, towards evening, the king having set up a battery opposite that of the enemy, they were, in their turn, obliged to withdraw their cavalry. By three or four in the afternoon the whole of our army was encamped.

As soon as it had settled down the king began to reconnoitre the hostile camp and the fords of the river. During the whole time the artillery was directing its fire against us, with little loss to us, it is true, but to the great danger of the king. Posterity may have difficulty in believing how this great prince escaped with his life. It must be mentioned that the enemy, having perceived through their field glasses that the king was reconnoitring their camp, and advancing towards the bank of the river in order to reconnoitre the fords, pointed their artillery at the group. The second shot which they fired – it was from a 6-pounder – almost overthrew the king. The ball passed so near his back that his doublet, his waistcoat, and his coat were burnt about a hand's breadth, and the skin grazed so closely that it bled . . . Those about His Majesty thought he was dangerously wounded, but he said with great coolness, 'It is nothing; but the ball came very near.' . . . The king then asked for his cloak, in order to hide the hole burnt in his coat, and went on further. After having received this wound, he remained two or three hours longer on horseback, lest the report that he was wounded should spread through the camp and alarm the troops. Having reached the extremity of the trenches he retired into his tent. The doctors wished to bleed him. He laughed at them, and called for his own surgeon, who applied a plaster to the wound. After this the king put on another coat, again mounted his horse, and went out to visit the lines. Meanwhile a report had spread amongst the troops that the king was dangerously wounded, and, as they did not know at what time he had received the wound, they had no idea that they had seen him since the occurrence. So great was their joy at beholding him appear on horseback, that the whole camp rang with acclamations and with cries of 'God save the king!' At the same instant similar shouts were heard in the hostile camp. We have since been informed that they were occasioned by a speech which King James had delivered to his troops. He exhorted them to fight bravely, and assured them that he would himself fight at their head. Seeing both sides thus determined to show their mettle, we expected a bloody engagement. . . .

The Duke of Schomberg, and with him several English generals, maintained that the best plan would be to make a false attack in the direction of the river, and thus draw the enemy's attention to that quarter; to send the best part of the army across the river during the night, at a ford some four or five miles distant to the right of the camp, and to attack the enemy in flank, so that they, being thus hemmed in between the river and that part of the army which had crossed it, should find it difficult to extricate themselves with any advantage. The second plan, which was supported by Count Solms, was to attack the enemy in front, to cross the river in their teeth, and force a passage through them. This opinion appeared to the king bolder than the former, and was, perhaps, more to his taste and in accordance with his enterprising character, but he thought it less safe. He adopted a middle course between these two extreme opinions.

It was resolved that Count Meynard Schomberg, at the head of the greater part of the cavalry, should cross the river at break of day at the ford which I have mentioned above as being four or five miles distant from the camp; that he should endeavour to meet the enemy at about nine in the morning, and that, at the same moment, the king with the main body of the army, should attack the enemy in front and force a passage across the river. The time was fixed at between eight and nine because the tide would then be at its ebb and the fords passable. When this had been settled the king gave orders that the army should retire to rest and should be under arms by daybreak next morning....

Yesterday morning [*1 July*], at break of day Count Meynard Schomberg, at the head of six or seven thousand horse and a few battalions of foot, was detached from the main body, in accordance with the plans previously formed. He crossed the river at the spot which had been fixed upon, on our right and the enemy's left. He encountered the hostile troops at about half-past nine. The engagement was not of long duration, for they at once gave way, and he pursued them hotly for a considerable time. The king, accurately conjecturing from the enemy's movements that they were being attacked by Count Meynard, laid his infantry across the river. The regiment of Dutch Guards was the first that crossed, the men being above their waists in water. The enemy occupied a village which stands on the bank of a river, and about which there are small gardens enclosed by hedges. The Dutch rushed to the attack with such impetuosity, that their opponents immediately abandoned their position, and our men, after having pursued them for some time, drew themselves up in battle array, in order to maintain the ground which they had gained.

A moment later three squadrons of King James's body-guard, which appeared to us to be very determined, rushed sword in hand upon this regiment, to the support of which a regiment of French refugees and some English regiments were hastening. It defended itself with so much bravery, that the Irish were twice obliged to retire with great loss, and the Dutch remained masters of the position.

The Duke of Schomberg, who had not yet crossed the river, and who was standing on an eminence, seeing that, if King James's body-guard returned to the charge, the Dutch regiment might be overthrown, hastened to bring it assistance by urging the regiments above mentioned, together with several squadrons of cavalry, to cross over in all speed. To ensure the success of the manoeuvre he crossed over himself. Scarcely had he reached the opposite bank when King James's body-guard returned to the charge for the third time, and with such intrepidity that it at length succeeded in breaking the lines of the Dutch regiment, which had not yet been able to receive assistance from the troops despatched for this purpose. They were, however, already in the river, and were firing from a distance on the Irish, who, urged on by too great a zeal, had rashly ventured as far as the street of the village. This gave us an opportunity of cutting them off, so that very few remained, and our troops were left masters of the position. But in the confusion caused by this charge, the Duke of Schomberg, who had been recognized by the king's guards, most likely from his blue ribbon, received two sabre wounds on the head at the same time as he was struck in the neck by a bullet from a carbine, fired, as it is presumed, by our own men, who were crossing the river and discharging their pieces as they advanced. The shot threw the duke from his horse. He fell on a very stony path, and this doubtless contributed to hasten the great man's death. Thus died this illustrious general at the age of eighty-two...

Whilst this was going on, the king was sending the remaining troops across the river at various spots. The enemy were driven back from all the posts which they occupied along the river with but little loss to our side....[6]

On learning that the Duke of Schomberg had been killed, William himself crossed the Boyne on horseback.

As soon as the king had crossed the river, the enemy were pressed with more vigour [*the Danish report continues*]. The king himself led the cavalry to the charge, having nothing but a walking stick in his hand, not having been able to put on his cuirass because of the wound which he had received the day before. Several squadrons behind which he rode were more than once repulsed, and he was three or four times in danger of being taken, and numberless times of being killed as easily as a simple foot soldier...

Meantime Count Schomberg was still in pursuit of the enemy; but as he had no orders to cut them off, and as the king on his side was not pressing them so closely as he might have done, perhaps wishing to put into practice Caesar's maxim, and 'leave his enemy's a golden bridge', they were able to retire. This they did in great haste and confusion, but with greater loss from deserters than from killed. . . .

In spite of the promises which he had given his army, King James was the first to take to flight. He only saw the beginning of the action. As soon as he saw that a part of our troops had crossed the river, he thought of his own safety. The reiterated proofs of weakness which he gave and the terror which took possession of him contributed in no small degree to the overthrow of his troops.[6]

Many Irishmen that day were humiliated by the manner of their defeat, and expressed a wish that the kings could have reversed sides. John Stevens, a lieutenant in James's army, wrote in his journal for 1 July:

We had this morning received advice that the enemy marching by night had beaten off a regiment of our dragoons that guarded the bridge of Slane and possessed themselves of it, and now we saw them marching off from their right towards it. We on the other side marched from the left, the river being between both: for a considerable space we marched under the enemy's cannon, which they played furiously without any intermission, yet did but little execution. We continued marching along the river till coming in sight of the enemy who had passed it and were drawing up, we marched off to the left as well to leave ground for them that followed to draw up, as to extend our line equal with theirs, and finding them still stretching out towards their right we held on our march to the left. Being thus in expectation of advancing to engage, news was brought us that the enemy, having endeavoured to gain the pass we had left behind, were repulsed with considerable loss on both sides, the Lord Dungan, a colonel of dragoons, and many brave men of ours being killed. The latter part was true, the former so far from it that they gained the ford, having done much execution on some of our foot that at first opposed them and quite broke such of our horse as came to rescue the foot, in which action the horse guards and Colonel Parker's regiment of horse behaved themselves with unspeakable bravery, but not being seconded and overpowered by the enemy, after having done what men could do, they were forced to save their remains by flight, which proved fatal to the foot. For the horse in general, taking their flight towards the left, broke the whole line of the foot, riding over all our battalions. The Lord Grand Prior's wherein I served were then in Duleek Lane, enclosed with high banks, marching ten in rank. The horse came on so unexpected and with such speed, some firing their pistols, that we had no time to receive or shun them, but all supposing them to be the enemy (as indeed they were no better to us) took to their heels, no officer being able to stop the men even after they were broken, and the horse passed, though at the same time no enemy was near us or them that fled in such haste to our destruction....

The first cause I had to suspect the route at the ford was that the Duke of Berwick, whose command was with the horse, came to us and discovering a party of horse at a distance, thinking they were the enemy, commanded our musketeers to line the side of the bank over which they appeared, till finding they were our own men we continued our march....

I thought the calamity had not been so general till viewing the hills about us I perceived them covered with soldiers of several regiments, all scattered like sheep flying before the wolf, but so thick they seemed to cover the sides and tops of the hills. The shame of our regiment's dishonour only afflicted me before; but now all the horror of a routed army, just before so vigorous and desirous of battle and broke without scarce a stroke from the enemy, so perplexed my soul that I envied the few dead, and only grieved I lived to be a spectator of so dismal and lamentable a tragedy. Scarce a regiment was left but what was reduced to a very inconsiderable number by this, if possible, more than panic fear. Only the French can be said to have rallied, for only they made head against the enemy, and a most honourable retreat, bringing off their cannon, and marching in very good order after sustaining the shock of the enemy who thereupon made a halt, not only to the honour of the French but the preservation of the rest of the scattered army.[44]

James had about 1,600 men killed, wounded, or captured; William's casualties were about five hundred. As battles go, not a large one; but it was decisive. From that moment the reconquest of Ireland was assured.

William made a ceremonial entry into Dublin, went south and secured the important port of Waterford, then west, crossing the country to put Limerick under siege. He first planned to direct the crossing of the Shannon, then leave responsibility for the siege of Limerick to Count Solms. He changed his mind on the easy crossing of the Shannon; but in marching on Limerick heavy rains fell, and a portion of his artillery were surprised by Patrick Sarsfield. Limerick was defended with great fervour and courage. In attempting to storm the town, though they made a breach in the walls, William's advance party was cut off and suffered heavy losses.

William's chaplain, the Rev. George Storey, describes the disastrous attack on Limerick:

Wednesday the 27th (August) . . . About half an hour after three the signal being given by firing three pieces of cannon, the Grenadiers being in the furthest angle of our trenches leapt over and ran towards the counterscarp firing their pieces and throwing their grenades. This gave the alarm to the Irish, who had their guns all ready, and discharged great and small shot up at us as fast as 'twas possible. Our men were not behind them in either; so that in less than two minutes the noise was so terrible that one would have thought the very skies ready to rent in sunder. This was seconded with dust, smoke, and all the terrors that the art of man could invent, to ruin and undo one another; and to make it the more uneasy, the day itself was excessive hot to the bystanders, and much more sure in all respects to those upon action. . . .

The Irish then ventured upon the breach again, and from the walls and every place so pestered us upon the counterscarp, that after nigh three hours resisting bullets, stones (broken bottles from the very women, who boldly stood in the breach, and were nearer our men than their own), and whatever ways could be thought on to destroy us, our ammunition being spent, it was judged safest to return to our trenches. When the work was at the hottest, the Brandenburgh Regiment (who behaved themselves very well) were got upon the black battery, where the enemy's powder happened to take fire, and blew up a great many of them, the men, faggots, stones, and what not, flying into the air with a most terrible noise. . . . The

Danes were not idle all this while, but fired upon the enemy with all imaginable fury, and had several killed; but the mischief was we had one breach, and all towards the left it was impossible to get into the town when the gates were shut [even] if there had been no enemy to oppose us, without a great many scaling-ladders, which we had not. From half an hour after three, till after seven, there was one continued fire of both great and small shot, without any intermission; in so much that the smoke that went from the town reached in one continued cloud to the top of a mountain at least six miles off. . . .

The King stood nigh Cromwell's fort all the time, and the business being over, he went to the camp very much concerned, as indeed was the whole Army; for you might have seen a mixture of anger and sorrow on everybody's countenance. . . . We lost at least five hundred upon the spot, and had a thousand more wounded, as I understood by the surgeons of our hospitals, who are the properest judges. The Irish lost a great many by our cannon and other ways; but it cannot be supposed that their loss should be equal to ours, since it's a much easier thing to defend walls, than 'tis by plain strength to force people from them. . . .

Next day the King sent a drummer, in order to a truce, that the dead might be buried, but the Irish had no mind to it; and now the soldiers were in hopes that the King would make a second attack, and seemed resolved to have the Town or die every man. But this was too great a hazard to run at one place, and they did not know how scarce our ammunition was, it being very much wasted the day before. This day however we continued battering the wall, and it began to rain; the next day it was very cloudy all about, and rained very fast, so that everybody began to dread the consequences of it. The King therefore called a Council of War, wherein it was resolved to quit the Town and raise the siege, which as the case stood then with us, was no doubt the most prudent thing that could be done. . . . Therefore, on Sunday the last of August, all the army drew off, (having a good body of horse in the rear). As soon as the Irish perceived we had quitted our trenches, they soon took possession of them with great joy, and were in a small time after over all the ground whereon we had encamped.[47]

Lieutenant John Stevens, ashamed in defeat at the Boyne, had cause for pride at the defence of Limerick.

26: The day began as usual with the noise of the cannon from all the enemy's batteries. This day they perfected their intended work, having made a breach in the southernmost part of the east wall near twenty paces wide, and though somewhat high yet easy of ascent, the vast quantity of rubbish beaten from the upper part of the wall and tower having almost filled the counterscarp so that there was no difficulty in mounting. . . .

27th: The enemy's batteries played furiously, the furthest off being the least at Ball's Bridge, the great one at the breach till they had laid it open above thirty paces and made the ascent plainer on their side than it was from the town. . . . Before we could come up the running we perceived the breach possessed by the enemy, a great number came down into the retrenchment made within it and above twenty of them were got into the street. Having heard no firing of small shot before, we at the first sight thought they had been our guards retiring out of the counterscarp, they being all in red coats, till we discovered the green boughs in their hats which was the mark of distinction worn by the rebels, whereas ours was white paper. Besides an officer on the breach brandishing his sword called upon his men to follow, crying the town was their own. . . .

Meanwhile the Grand Prior's Regiment had well lined the retrenchment within the breach, and, being undeceived that the enemy and not our own men were those that rushed in so impetuous, the word was given to fire, which was performed so effectually that a considerable number of the rebels dropped, and our men renewed their charges with such vigour that in a very short space they had not left one enemy within the breach, though still nothing daunted they pressed over, fresh men succeeding those that were killed or wounded.

This sort of fight was continued near an hour, our battalion alone making good their ground against that multitude of enemies which being still backed with new supplies was all that while insensible to its losses. . . . Our continual fire having made a great slaughter among the rebels and they beginning to abate of their first fury, M. de Beaupré, a Frenchman, and Lieutenant-Colonel Boisseleau, our

Governor, leaped over our retrenchment making to the breach. Most men strove to be foremost in imitating so good an example, so that being followed by a resolute party he soon recovered the top of the breach. Here the fight was for some time renewed and continued with sword in hand and the butt end of the muisket. Our other men upon the walls were not idle this while, some firing and others casting stones upon the enemy beneath, which did no small execution, but the greatest havoc was made by two pieces of cannon playing from the citadel and two others from the king's island, as also two others on the Augustine chapel near Ball's Bridge, which last scoured all along our counterscarp then filled with rebels, and the other four swept them in their approach from the south and east sides. The enemy thus cut off on all sides came on fatally, and a barrel of powder which lay near the south-east tower accidently taking fire and blowing up some that were near it, the rest conceived it had been a mine and fled. . . . The action continued hot and dubious for at least three hours, and, above half an hour after, went in diminution till the enemy wholly drew off. A great slaughter was made of them . . .

Saturday, 30th. This morning we observed there was great silence in the enemy's works and day appearing we could not perceive anybody in them, which at first was looked upon as a stratagem to draw us out of our works, but some few being sent out to discover returned and brought the news that all abroad was clear. Immediately the word was carried about all our works that the rebels had raised the siege and stole away in the dead of night, which at first seemed incredible to many. In a short space our men could not be contained within the works but running out found the enemy's works and trenches abandoned, and their dead lying everywhere in great numbers unburied, being those that were killed at the assault. . . . There were infinite numbers of crows and ravens, which seemed to have resorted from all parts of the country to prey upon the dead bodies that lay everywhere unburied. They were with the plenty of of food grown excessively fat, which made them appear above the common size, and so tame that they walked among men familiarly as home-bred fowls do.[44]

The siege of Limerick lifted, 30 August 1690, William returned to London. The Irish and French continued the fight for more than a year, though victory for William was certain. During the autumn of 1690 Marlborough took Cork and Kinsale from the sea, and during the summer of 1691 Ginckel took Athlone, Aughrim, and Limerick. Patrick Sarsfield, respected as an opponent by William and his generals, stubbornly defended Limerick during its second siege, and negotiated terms before surrendering on 3 October 1691.

By the terms of the treaty of Limerick, James's Irish soldiers were given the opportunity to leave Ireland: fourteen thousand sailed to the Continent, where they fought for France and other Catholic countries in Europe. Sarsfield was killed at the battle of Landen in Flanders in 1693, with, it was said, the dying words: 'Would it were for Ireland.'

With the soldiers went thousands of Catholic gentry who had supported James. The 'flight of the wild geese' as it is known led to a further transferring of land from Catholic to Protestant ownership. In 1688 Catholics held twenty-two per cent of cultivable land in Ireland; in 1703, after the Williamite settlement, they held fifteen per cent.

'It is difficult if not impossible to fit him into the history of any single nation,' says William's most recent biographer (Stephen B. Baxter: William III, Longmans Green, 1966). 'Dutch historians have held their Prince in high regard, but they have not felt him to be a very good Dutchman. English historians have been content to think of him as a foreigner, as Dutch William.' But many thousands of Ulster Protestants revere his 'glorious, pious, and immortal memory' – and in some respects for reasons with which he would have had no sympathy. William was no anti-Catholic bigot: the mass was said daily in the chapel of his château at Orange; he made sure that tolerance was shown to Catholics in England; and his taming of the power-mad Louis XIV had the support of Catholic Leopold of Austria – and the Pope. In its setting as part of a European struggle, of which William's Irish campaign was but a part, the result of the Battle of the Boyne was received with jubilation in the Vatican. (The Unionist government of Northern Ireland once purchased at considerable cost a contemporary portrait of William III, which also depicted some of his European allies: it was only after cleaning that one of the figures *was seen to be the Pope. Though embarrassing questions were asked in Parliament, what became of the painting remains a mystery.)*

Yet, in the Irish context, one can understand the significance for Orangemen in celebrating William's victory at the Boyne; for the defeat of the Catholic King James marks the birth of the Protestant Ascendancy in Ireland. James II was the last Catholic king of England: with the Protestant throne and Protestant Church secured, and with Catholics thereafter a small minority in the country, religious contentions had henceforth little or no place in the lives of Englishmen. It was very different in Ireland, where Catholics and Protestants had each found unity and a separate identity: the divisions thus polarized have bedevilled Irish life for three centuries.

The French are on the sea, says the Shan Van Vocht;
The French are in the Bay, they'll be here without delay,
And the Orange will decay, says the Shan Van Vocht.
> *The Shan Van Vocht.*

This is a most wretched country. The upper orders have fallen into a lethargy, and are only occupied in eating and drinking, or in uttering their unmanly fears. They know that they have been the oppressors of the poor, and that the moment of vengeance is at hand.
> General Sir Ralph Abercromby, Commander-in-Chief of the Irish Army, in a letter to his son dated 1st April 1798.

A wet winter, a dry spring,
A bloody summer, and no King.
> Irish prophecy for 1798.

Enniscorthy's in flames, and old Wexford is won,
And the Barrow tomorrow we cross,
On a hill o'er the town we have planted a gun
That will batter the gateways of Ross!
All the Forth men and Bargy men will march o'er the heath
With brave Harvey to lead on the van;
But foremost of all in the grim Gap of Death
Will be Kelly, the Boy from Killanne!
> *Kelly of Killane.*

The Rebellion of 1798

One might have expected Irish support for the Jacobite rebellions of 1715 and 1745. None was forthcoming, and reasons are not hard to find. Following the Treaty of Limerick, 14,000 Catholic soldiers had left Ireland to fight for Catholic countries on the Continent, and most of the leaders of the remaining Old Irish and Old English similarly emigrated. This loss of fighting men and educated leaders subdued the Catholic revolutionary spirit for a century. In addition, Catholics were subjected to penal laws that reduced them to social and political impotence.

All the signs are that William genuinely wished to be generous to the Catholics and to honour the terms offered them in the Treaty of Limerick – rights of worship 'as are consistent with the laws of Ireland, or as they did enjoy in the reign of King Charles II'. That the treaty was not honoured was due to powerful Protestant pressures from Ireland and from the English Establishment, which, beginning in William's reign and continued in those of Anne and the first two Georges, forced through a series of Acts, known as the Penal Laws, suppressing Irish Catholics and having the effect of maintaining the ascendancy of the Protestant class, composing about a quarter of the population of Ireland. Among things forbidden to Catholics were: standing for parliament or local councils, or voting for those who did; holding positions in the civil service, on civic boards, or in law, or commissions in the army or navy; manufacturing or selling books or newspapers; taking out or giving mortgages; owning arms, or a horse worth more than five pounds; marrying a Protestant. They could not have their own schools, teach, or send their children abroad to be educated. The ownership of land by Catholics was hedged around with restraints and restrictions. When a Catholic died, his estate was to be divided amongst all his children; but a son who became a Protestant inherited his father's entire estate. Registered priests were tolerated, but not bishops, archbishops, or cardinals. In short: all positions of power and prestige were denied to Catholics.

The penal laws were not strictly enforced. Many Catholics found ways to get round them, sometimes with the connivance of friendly Protestants. The historian Sir George Clark wrote: 'The Protestants regarded the code not as laying down the exact condition to which they would reduce the Catholics; but as giving them a reserve of power, an armoury of weapons to which they might resort at need. There was, however, sufficient enforcement to effect the main purpose of the laws, and the existence of the reserve of power continually aided in this. The Catholic population acquired the qualities of a subject population.' Despite the harsh anti-Catholic laws, thousands of priests, monks, and nuns actively propagated their faith in Ireland during the time of the penal laws. An all-out attempt to suppress the Catholic religion was never made.

In contrast to the depressed nature of the Catholic population, the minority Protestant ascendancy-class asserted themselves in a flowering of a Protestant Irish nationalism, with which the name of Jonathan Swift, Dean of St Patrick's Cathedral, Dublin, is always associated. His incisive power with words was directed against injustices wherever he saw them. He was joined by another Protestant divine, George Berkeley, philosopher Bishop of Cloyne, in considering the laws against Catholics an outrage upon justice. Swift never claimed to be a patriot – his voice was raised, he said, 'owing to the perfect rage and resentment, and the mortifying sight of slavery, folly, and baseness about me, among which I am forced to live.' – but he helped create a climate of opinion in which a united Protestant/Catholic nationalism could grow.

Swift supported the two causes on which the ascendancy-class flexed their muscles: legislative independence and free trade. They resented the subservience of the Irish parliament to that in London. In 1719 the Declaratory Act reaffirmed the right – first introduced during the reign of Henry VII, Poynings' Law – of the British parliament to legislate for Ireland. In a pamphlet published in Dublin in 1728, Swift wrote:

It is too well known that we are forced to obey some laws we never consented to ... Thus, we are in the condition of patients who have physic sent them by doctors at a distance, strangers to their constitution, and the nature of their disease.[48]

On the second great grievance, Swift wrote:

Ireland is the only Kingdom I ever heard or read of, either in ancient or modern story, who is denied the liberty of exporting their native commodities or manufactures wherever they pleased, except the countries at war with their own Prince or State, yet this by the superiority of mere power is refused us in the most momentous parts of commerce, besides an Act of Navigation to which we never consented, pinned down upon us, and rigorously executed, and a thousand other unexampled circumstances as grievous as they are invidious to mention.[48]

The ruffled Protestants found skilful parliamentary leaders in two lawyers: Henry Flood and Henry Grattan. The constitutional battle was prolonged, but in 1780 England lifted restrictions on Irish trade, and two years later Ireland was given legislative independence, though a Lord-Lieutenant remained at the head of the administration. The spirit of independence among Irish Protestants had been boosted by the success of the American colonists in opposing the Crown. In 1782 the Irish parliament had actually passed a Declaration of Independence. Grattan's prime aim seemed achieved: Great Britain and Ireland independent nations in 'constitutional confederacy' under a joint Crown. But in practice, the system of patronage kept the Irish legislature bound to English interests.

It was a victory for Protestants only: Catholics were still excluded from Parliament. Catholic Emancipation, as it was called, became the big parliamentary issue for the remainder of the century. The result of freedom of trade and other concessions to greater Irish independence brought a period of rising prosperity that left a reminder in some of the fine Georgian architecture seen today in Dublin. But the living conditions of the peasantry, meaning the mass of the people, were scarcely touched – 'wretched' was the description most often used by author-travellers. Swift's description of fifty years before still applied:

The miserable dress, and diet, and dwelling of the people. . . . The families of farmers who pay great rents, living in filth and nastiness upon buttermilk and potatoes, without a shoe or stocking to their feet, or a house so convenient as an English hog-sty to receive them. . . . The rise of our rents is squeezed out of the very blood and vitals, and clothes, and dwellings of the tenants who live worse than English beggars.[48]

The relationship between landlord and tenant did not bode well for a peaceful future. Arthur Young toured Ireland in 1776, and observed:
A landlord in Ireland can scarcely invent an order which a servant, labourer or cottar dares to refuse to execute. Nothing satisfies him but an unlimited submission. . . . The execution of the law lies very much in the hands of justices of the peace, many of whom are drawn from the most illiberal class in the kingdom. If a poor man lodges a complaint against a gentleman, and the justice issues out a summons for his appearance, it is a fixed affront, and he will infallibly be called out. Where manners are in conspiracy against law, to whom are the oppressed people to have recourse?[55]

Thousands turned for recourse to agrarian secret societies, and after 1791 to the Society of United Irishmen, which began as an open reformist movement opposing English domination, but which rapidly became underground, revolutionary, and republican, and the driving force behind the great rebellion of 1798.

The origin of the movement can be traced to the Volunteer clubs of the previous decade, which gave many of the United Irish leaders some feeling for soldiering. The Irish Volunteers were formed in 1778 on the withdrawal of troops from Ireland to fight the rebel colonists in America. By the end of 1781 they had about eighty thousand men, and their convention at Dungannon in 1782 was a powerful display of strength that helped force the English parliament to renounce the right of the English government to legislate for Ireland. The Volunteers were Protestants; Catholics could not hold arms. It was out of the radicalism of the northern Volunteer clubs that the Society of United Irishmen was born.

The involvement of Ulster's Presbyterians in separatist republicanism looks strange today, but in the late eighteenth century Belfast was the centre where radical ideas were most debated and propagated and where the French Revolution made greatest impact in Ireland. Two points are worth noting: firstly, as Nonconformists or Dissenters, Presbyterians had suffered certain disabilities arising from the penal code against Catholics; secondly, Presbyterian emigrants from Ulster were in the forefront of the American colonists' fight for independence and in the shaping and management of the new nation, about a dozen American Presidents would be of 'Scotch-Irish' blood.

In 1791 a twenty-eight-year-old Dublin barrister, Theobald Wolfe Tone, who had written a pamphlet addressed principally to the Irish Dissenters, pleading to them to 'forget all former feuds, to consolidate the entire strength of the whole nation and to form for the future but one people', travelled to Belfast for the founding of the Society of United Irishmen; similar organizations followed in Dublin and in many parts of Ireland. Tone's ancestry, family background, and personal history give no clue to his becoming Ireland's leading revolutionary: descended from one of Cromwell's soldiers; his parents Protestant middle class; educated at Trinity College, Dublin, the establishment university; his first involvement in politics when he submitted to Downing Street a plan to colonize the islands discovered by Captain Cook in the South Seas so as to curb Spain's power. But soon he was developing radical ideas, and like many young men of the Protestant professional class in Ireland was bowled over by the impact of the French Revolution (1789) and its clarion cries of Liberty, Equality, and Fraternity.

The United Irishmen knew that for a successful insurrection they needed the support of the Catholic peasantry: they found a ready response among members of a Catholic secret society called the Defenders, also influenced by the French revolutionary ideas.

Any alliance between radical Protestants and Catholics was a perturbing sight to the British government, and, facing the threat of France, Prime Minister Pitt favoured some form of conciliation with the Catholics. He persuaded the Irish parliament to relax most of the penal laws – but they drew the line at permitting Catholics the emancipation of sitting with Protestants in parliament. When Pitt appointed Lord Fitzwilliam Viceroy in January 1795, Irish Catholic hopes rose, only to be dashed when he was soon recalled to London and replaced by Lord Camden. A polarization between radicals and reactionaries, between revolutionary and constitutional separatism, was complete – a bifurcation lasting up to our own times.

The first arrests of United Irishmen began in 1793, the year war broke out between Britain and France. Wolfe Tone was expelled to America in 1795, whence he moved to France, where he successfully pleaded with the directory for a large expedition to sail to Ireland, where, Tone assured them, the people were on the brink of revolution.

At night, on 16th December 1796, a French fleet of forty-five ships, carrying about 14,750 men, commanded by General Lazare Hoche, evaded a British squadron blockading Brest, and sailed for Ireland. Tone, in the uniform of a French adjutant-general, was on board the 80-gun flagship, the Indomptable. The plan was on a grand scale, and could have altered the course of both Irish and British history if they had landed. The aim was to force out the English, and set up an Irish Republic, from which England would be conquered or through revolution also become a republic. In avoiding the British blockade, the French fleet had split up – when on the 21st thirty-five ships, carrying 12,000 men reached Bantry Bay, the frigate carrying General Hoche was missing. As they waited for his arrival, the wind which had aided their crossing turned against them: more than half the fleet separated from the flagship. A storm blew up on the 24th, forcing the Indomptable and other French ships to cut their cables. During the night of the 27th it blew a hurricane, scattering the invasionary fleet and Tone's expectations. His journal offers a prologue of the rebellion of 1798, an operatic scena of which Verdi might have made much.

December 25. Last night I had the strongest expectations that today we should debark, but at two this morning I was awakened by the wind. I rose immediately, and wrapping myself in my great coat, walked for an hour in the gallery, devoured by the most gloomy reflections. The wind continues right ahead, so that it is absolutely impossible to work up to the landing place, and God knows when it will change. The same wind is exactly favourable to bring the English upon us, and these cruel delays give the enemy time to assemble his entire force in this neighbourhood . . . if we are taken, my fate will not be a mild one; the best I can expect is to be shot as an *emigré rentré*, unless I have the good fortune to be killed in action; for most assuredly if the enemy will have us, he must fight for us. Perhaps I may be reserved for a trial, for the sake of striking terror into others, in which case I shall be hanged as a traitor and embowelled, etc. As to the embowelling, *'je m'en fiche'*, if ever they hang me, they are welcome to embowel me if they please. These are pleasant prospects! Nothing on earth could sustain me now, but the consciousness that I am engaged in a just and righteous cause. For my family, I have, by a desperate effort, surmounted my natural feelings so far, that I do not think of them at this moment. . . .

December 26. Certainly we have been persecuted by a strange fatality . . . We have lost two commanders-in-Chief; of four admirals not one remains; we have lost one ship of the line that we know of, and probably many others of which we know nothing; we have been now six days in Bantry Bay, within five hundred yards of the shore, without being able to effectuate a landing; we have been dispersed four times in four days; and at this moment, of forty-three sail, of which the expedition consisted, we can muster of all sizes but fourteen. There only wants our falling in with the English to complete our destruction. . . .

December 27. Yesterday several vessels, including the *Indomptable*, dragged their anchors several times, and it was with great difficulty they rode out the gale. At two o'clock, the *Revolution*, a seventy-four, made signal that she could hold no longer, and in consequence of the commodore's permission who now commands our little squadron, cut her only cable and put to sea. In the night, the *Patriote* and *Pluton*, of seventy-four each, were forced to put to sea with the Nicomede flute, so that this morning we are reduced to seven sail of the line and one frigate. Any attempt here is now desperate; but I think still, if we were debarked at the mouth of the Shannon, we might yet recover all . . . At half after four, there being every appearance of a stormy night, three vessels cut their cables and put to sea. The *Indomptable*, having with great difficulty weighed anchor, we were forced, at length, to cut the cable of the other, and make the best of our way out of the bay, being followed by the whole of our little squadron, now reduced to ten sail, of which seven are of the line, one frigate, and two corvettes or luggers.

December 28. Last night it blew a perfect hurricane. At one this morning a dreadful sea took the ship in the quarter, stove in the quarter gallery, and one of the dead-lights in the great cabin, which was instantly filled with water to the depth of three feet. The cots of the officers were almost all torn down, and themselves and their trunks floated about the cabin. For my part, I had just fallen asleep when awakened by the shock, of which I at first did not comprehend the meaning; but hearing the water distantly rolling in the cabin beneath me, and two or three of the officers mounting in their shirts as wet as if they had risen from the bottom of the sea, I concluded instantly that the ship had struck and was filling with water, and that she would sink directly. . . . Immediately after this blow, the wind abated, and at daylight, having run nine knots an hour under one jib only, during the hurricane, we found ourselves at the rendezvous, having parted company with three ships of the line, and the frigate, which makes our *sixth* separation. The frigate *Coquille* joined us in the course of the day, which we spent standing off and on the shore, without being joined by any of our missing companions.

December 29. At four this morning, the commodore made the signal to steer for France; so there is an end of our expedition for the present; perhaps for ever.[51]

There was a repeat frustration for Tone in July of the following year. Gales had prevented the French expedition landing in December 1796; in 1797 a fleet and invasionary force – fifteen sail of the line, ten frigates and sloops, and twenty-seven transports – raised by France's ally the Dutch Republic, were becalmed in the North Sea port of Texel, at a time when the British fleet was crippled by mutinies at the Nore and Spithead. A kind of existentialist apathy permeates Tone's journal –
'*For our expedition I think no more of it than if it were destined for Japan*' *– yet this repeated opposition of the elements was too much:*

Eighteen days aboard and we have not had eighteen minutes of fair wind. Hell! Hell! Hell! Allah! Allah! Allah![51]

In mid-August the 13,500 Dutch troops were disembarked, and Tone posted to General Hoche's staff in Belgium. There were further blows for Tone. Hoche, who had befriended Tone and done much to press the Irish cause with the Directory, died suddenly of consumption in September. And in October, when the Dutch fleet came out from Texel, they were defeated by the British in a famous victory off Camperdown.

Tone had meetings with Napoleon in December 1797, but his plea that another French invasionary force should be sent to Ireland received a guarded response.

December 18, 19, 20, 21. General Desaix brought Lewines [*a Dublin solicitor*] and me this morning and introduced us to Buonaparte, at his house in the Rue Chantereine. He lives in the greatest simplicity; his house is small but neat, and all the furniture and ornaments in the most classical taste. He is about five feet six inches high, slender, and well made, but stoops considerably; he looks at least ten years older than he is, owing to the great fatigues he underwent in his immortal campaign of Italy. His face is that of a profound thinker, but bears no marks of that great enthusiasm and unceasing activity by which he has been so much distinguished. It is rather, to my mind, the countenance of a mathematician than of a General. He has a fine eye, and a great firmness about his mouth; he speaks low and hollow. So much for his manner and figure. We had not much discourse with him, and what little there was, was between him and Lewines to whom, as our Ambassador, I gave the *pas*. We told him that Tennant was about to depart for Ireland, and was ready to charge himself with his orders if he had any to give. He desired us to bring him the same evening, and so we took our leave.

In the evening we returned with Tennant, and Lewines had a good deal of conversation with him; that is to say Lewines insensed him a good deal on Irish affairs, of which he appears a good deal uninformed: for example, he seems convinced that our population is not more than two million, which is nonsense. Buonaparte listened, but said very little. When all this was finished, he desired that Tennant might put off his departure for a few days....

December 23. Called this evening on Buonaparte, by appointment, with Tennant and Lewines, and saw him for about five minutes. Lewines gave him a copy of the memorials I delivered to the Government in February 1796 (nearly two years ago), and which, fortunately, have been well verified in every material fact, by everything that has taken place in Ireland since. He also gave him Taylor's map, and showed him half a dozen of Hoche's letters, which Buonaparte read over. He then desired us to return in two or three days, with such documents relating to Ireland which we were possessed of, and, in the meantime, that Tennant should postpone his departure. We then left him. His manner is cold, and he speaks very little; it is not, however, so dry as that of Hoche, but seems rather to proceed from languor than anything else. He is perfectly civil, however, to us; but, from anything we have seen or heard from him, it is impossible to augur anything good or bad. We have now seen the greatest man in Europe three times, and I am astonished to think how little I have to record about him.[51]

On 12 March 1798 an informer's tip-off led to the arrest of the fifteen members of the Leinster Committee of the United Irishmen. The news shattered Tone.

I have read news of the most disastrous and afflicting kind, as well for me individually, as for the country at large. The English Government has arrested the whole committee of United Irishmen for the province of Leinster, including almost every man I know and esteem in the city of Dublin. It is by far the most terrible blow which the cause of liberty in Ireland has yet sustained. I know not whether in the whole party it would be possible to replace the energy, talents, and integrity, of which we are deprived by this most unfortunate of events. I have not received such a shock from all that has passed since I left Ireland.[51]

One well-known United Irish leader remained at large. Lord Edward Fitzgerald, a Byronic revolutionary, who wore the plain brown suits and cropped hair style of the Jacobins, was to have become commander-in-chief of the rebel army. Eventually he was cornered in a feather-merchant's house in Dublin, where he stabbed to death a yeomanry captain before being overpowered, himself fatally wounded, and carried off in a sedan chair to the Castle. He died on 4 June, before he could be brought to trial.

The United Irishmen were now under fearsome pressure. W. H. Maxwell, who wrote a history of the '98 rebellion published in 1845, says: 'On the 30th of March, the kingdom was declared by proclamation to be "in actual rebellion", and the troops were directed to act without magisterial authority, whenever their own officers deemed it proper. That fearful order loosed a licentious soldiery upon the country, and every hope of averting bloodshed ended.'

A combination of severity and pardon had been operated by the military for over a year. Huge quantities of pikes and other arms had been handed in, or uncovered after the torture of suspects. The ruthlessness of search methods depended on the harshness or humanity of officers. At its most brutal, cabins were burned, men killed or maimed, suspects given hundreds of lashes with the cat-o'-nine-tails, half-hanged, or otherwise tortured in an attempt to make them reveal the names of United Irishmen or the hiding-place of arms. A frequent torture was the pitch-cap, mixed with gunpowder, squeezed down on the victim's head, and set alight.

General Sir Ralph Abercromby, Commander-in-Chief of the Irish Army, had caused a sensation by accusing his own army of atrocities in a general order issued on 26 February 1798, and of being 'in a state of licentiousness which must render it formidable to everyone but the enemy'. The Irish gentry saw Abercromby as a man who was soft on rebels and successfully pressed for his resignation. There was even talk of an impeachment. Lt-Gen. Gerard Lake, who succeeded Abercromby, was not inhibited by the latter's liberal scruples.

The rebellion broke out on 23 May, without support from the French, and with the most high-minded of the leaders in prison. Not only was strategic direction thus cut off from the rank and file, but also the philosophy of the movement. The leaders, if they had been at liberty, might have prevented at least some of the sectarian atrocities in Leinster that were totally at variance with United Irish ideals.

An officer with the royal army thus summed up the course of the rebellion during May:

If one can imagine such a thing as a *tableau*, or bird's-eye view of the rebellion from the 23rd to the 30th of May, the appearance it would present would be this. Seven or eight comparatively minor explosions, lighting up the atmosphere for a short space and then going gradually out, viz. one in Meath (Tara), one in Wicklow (Mount Kennedy), a good blaze in Carlow, and four or five in Kildare, which its being Lord Edward's own county accounts for – these were Naas, Prosperous, Kilcullen, and Rathangan. The eye should then be drawn to the mighty and absorbing eruption of Wexford....[1]

In concentrating within the space at our disposal, mainly on 'the mighty and absorbing eruption of Wexford', we will be where the fighting was fiercest and most critical for the government. Strangely, though Wexford was to provide the greatest threat to the Crown of any county in the rebellion, it had not been a hotbed of the United Irishmen, and thus had not received the repression suffered by some other counties, until it burst upon its people in terrible fury after the arrest of the Leinster Committee. An Arms Proclamation allowed fourteen days for the surrender of arms in Wexford; but there was no let up in the terror, whose chief exponents were the mainly Protestant yeomanry and the predominantly Catholic North Cork militia (inventors of the dreaded pitch-cap). In the view of some historians close to the times, the cruelty of the government forces pressed thousands of the peasantry into armed revolt. 'No one slept in his own house,' wrote Thomas Cloney of this time of fear. 'The very whistling of the birds seemed to report the approach of an enemy.'[13] On 26 May the rebellion in Wexford burst into flame. Thousands of peasants had taken to the fields, and became peasant armies. The largest force, led by Father John Murphy of Boulavogue, assembled on a hill at Oulart, ten miles south of Gorey and eight miles from Wexford town. Another rebel group assembled on Kilthomas Hill, nine miles west of Gorey, and was put to flight by three hundred yeomen from the garrison at Carnew, who in pursuit burned about a hundred cabins and farmhouses and two Roman Catholic churches, one of them Father Murphy's at Boulavogue. An attempt to dislodge the rebels on Oulart Hill was a disaster for a detachment of 109 men of the North Cork militia from the garrison at Wexford. Only Colonel Foote, commanding, a sergeant, and three privates returned to Wexford.

The rebels were elated by their success. Hundreds of them had melted away at the sight of the militia, but the main body, by standing their ground, had destroyed a detachment of the king's troops, killing over a hundred; no mercy was shown, no prisoners taken. As the wounded militia were piked to death, some waved missals and screamed that they too were Catholics. Four-fifths of the royal troops who put down the rising were Irish, the great majority Catholics.

The rebels now had the arms of the slaughtered militia. In high spirits, they marched for some hours about the countryside, unsure what to do next, but recruiting thousands of men, many of whom felt that as *the fury of the military was being directed against guilty and innocent alike, they might as well become insurgents. The huge, virtually leaderless peasant army finally decided to attack Enniscorthy, the second largest town in County Wexford. The garrison there consisted of eighty men of the North Cork militia and 200 local yeomanry. As the rebels attacked, they drove in front of them frightened cattle and horses – an ancient tactic they would repeat at New Ross. There was bloody hand-to-hand fighting in the streets. After three hours' fighting, the garrison had lost more than a hundred men, and at four o'clock in the afternoon the retreat was sounded, and the survivors took the road to Wexford, already crowded with refugees. The jubilant peasant army set up camp on Vinegar Hill, a prominence overlooking the town, most of the buildings of which were now burning.*

For several days thousands of Catholics made their way to Vinegar Hill to swell the ranks of the rebel army. One of these was Thomas Cloney, a young farmer, who felt it was the only course he could take. He survived the rebellion to write a level-headed and interesting memoir.

On Tuesday, the 29th of May, before day, a large body of men came to my father's house and pressed me to proceed with them to Enniscorthy. I put them off by promising to follow in a short time. Soon after another and a much more numerous party came, who were louder and more peremptory in their demands. There was now no time to be lost in deliberating. The innocent and guilty were alike driven into acts of unwilling hostility to the existing Government; but there was no alternative; every preceding day saw the instruments of torture filling the yawning sepulchres with the victims of suspicion or malice; and as a partial resistance could never tend to mitigate the cruelty of their tormentors, I saw no second course for me, or indeed for any Catholic in my part of the country, to pursue. I joined the people, and took an affectionate farewell of my father and sisters. . . .

On entering Enniscorthy, I perceived that the houses had continued burning, the slates were flying, impelled by the force of the flames, in all directions, and many dead bodies were lying in the streets scattered, and some of them mutilated. . . .

I ascended Vinegar Hill, wishing to turn my eyes from those

sickening objects which none but persons divested of all humanity could take pleasure in beholding. On the hill were assembled some thousands of people, inhabitants of that part of the county, north and north-east of Enniscorthy, many of whom bore evident marks of the dangers they had encountered in the two preceding days – some recounted the actions they had performed against the enemy, and showed wounds that proved them not destitute of courage; others mourned their children, brothers, relatives and friends, who fell in the late engagements, or who had suffered death previously by torture. More exclaimed that they were left without a house or home, their houses and property having been consumed by the Orange yeomanry. . . .[13]

With terror the norm, it was hardly surprising that the pattern familiar in Irish wars should be set from the start: atrocity and counter-atrocity, and the victim often marked not by his guilt or innocence, but by his religious persuasion. At Oulart 500 rebels surrounded the house of a Protestant clergyman, shooting him and piking to death seven of his parishioners who had taken refuge in the house. At Ballingale another Protestant clergyman and five of his parishioners were killed by insurgents. A windmill on top of Vinegar Hill was used as a lock-up for prisoners, said to have Orange sympathies, taken at Enniscorthy. A first batch were taken out and crudely executed with gun and pike on the Tuesday Thomas Cloney joined the camp. Yet to balance this grim picture, there were incidents in plenty of Catholics risking their lives to save those of Protestant neighbours, and vice versa. A Protestant clergyman who lived near Enniscorthy said: 'In justice I must allow that the rebels often displayed humanity and generosity deserving in praise and admiration.'

A Protestant woman, Mrs White, walked bravely into the rebel camp on Vinegar Hill seeking a written 'protection' for her family and house from a priest, Father Roche, who had joined the insurgents. The camp, she afterwards wrote . . .

. . . presented a dreadful scene of confusion and uproar. . . . Great numbers of women were in the camp. Some men were employed in killing cattle, and boiling them in pieces in large copper brewing-pans; others were drinking, cursing and swearing; many of them were playing on various musical instruments, which they had acquired by plunder in the adjacent Protestant houses ... the pikemen would often show us their pikes all stained with blood, and boast of having murdered our friends and neighbours.[53]

But Mrs White, unharmed, got her 'protection' from the priest.

'No man to molest this house, or its inhabitants, on pain of death.'

The absence of an overall plan was shown by the uncertainty of the force on Vinegar Hill as to what to do or where to go next, and by their move when it finally came. It had been a critical weekend for Ireland's rulers, and their troubles would have been much worse if the victors at Enniscorthy had marched north to link with the insurgents then active in Kildare and Wicklow, and so threaten Dublin itself. Gorey had been abandoned by its garrison, and the way to the north was open. In fact, the peasant army, after a few days indecision, marched south, with the intention of taking Wexford town. They camped for the night on a hill called Three Rocks, near the town. It was a still, warm night – the rebellion was fought in one of the driest and warmest summers in living memory. A prophecy for 1798 had been whispered among the peasantry:

> *A wet winter,*
> *A dry spring,*
> *A bloody summer,*
> *And no King.*

The first three predictions were accurate.

Thomas Cloney recalled the night the rebels camped at Three Rocks.

The night was very dark, and it was curious to hear the stragglers, or such as had separated from their respective bodies calling each other aloud by the names of their different baronies. Those calls in the stillness of a very calm summer's night, must have been distinctly heard by the out-posts of the garrison in Wexford, and from the names of so many baronies being incessantly repeated, the enemy was, no doubt, impressed with a strong notion of our having a greater numerical force than we really had, and they must have felt deep and powerful anxiety for the issue of the next day's expected attack.[13]

Charles Jackson, an English-born resident, describes the scenes of panic and confusion in Wexford on the afternoon of Monday 28 May:

... no description can give an adequate idea of the scene presented at Wexford. The inhabitants, who had escaped from Enniscorthy and its neighbourhood, pushed into the town in crowds; persons of the first fortunes, in that part of the country, covered with dust and blood, with their infants in their arms, and their wives clinging behind them; and such women, as had not been able to procure a horse or a seat with their husbands, endeavouring to keep up with the mob of fugitives, with their children in their arms and others hanging to them; women who, but a few hours before, were in possession of every comfort life could afford. The inhabitants of Wexford, still more terrified by the spectacle now before them, were each endeavouring to secure a berth for their wives and children on board some of the vessels lying in the harbour, every one of which was soon filled as full as it would hold. The gallant husbands and fathers now returned to their respective parades, apparently fortified with a double portion of courage, since the objects of their tenderest care seemed to have been placed in safety. The next morning, Tuesday, May 29, a party of the Donegal militia arrived, with two pieces of cannon, and brought news that more assistance was advancing; but, about twelve o'clock we received intelligence that a party of artillerymen, with cannon and howitzers, had been taken by the rebels. Orders were now given that all fires should be put out, and that such houses as had thatched roofs should be immediately stripped, to prevent the disaffected party from following the example of their associates at Enniscorthy, by setting fire to the town during the time of its being attacked.

On Wednesday, May 30, in the morning, the troops (the Donegal and Cork militia, near six hundred in all), went out to meet the rebels, who were now supposed to be fifteen thousand strong. About three miles from Wexford, at a place called Three Rocks, there was some firing, when the militia, finding them so powerful from numbers, and in possession of the artillery taken the day before, retreated to the town.

There were at this time, in the jail of Wexford, in consequence of an order from Dublin, Mr Beauchamp Bagenal Harvey, Mr Fitzgerald, and Mr Cokely [*Colclough, pronounced Cokely*], all men of property and of great interest in the county. A council was called, and it was resolved, that it was impossible to defend the town, as the greatest part of the Catholics who had taken up arms had deserted. The proportion of the Catholic inhabitants of Wexford I believe to have been about three to one Protestant, but only about two hundred had taken up arms; on the remainder, however, no dependence could be placed. Two gentlemen, Mr Richards, a counsellor, and Dr Jacobs [*Jacob*], a physician, mayor of the town, were appointed to offer to surrender the town to the rebels, and to endeavour to save the lives of the inhabitants; to which condition the rebels agreed. In the meantime, the troops, accompanied by all the unmarried yeomen, effected their escape to Duncannon Fort, about twenty-three miles off.[30]

On *31 May about fifteen thousand rebels marched triumphantly into Wexford. Charles Jackson thus described what little they had in the way of uniforms:*

The whole of the rebels wore white bands round their hats. Some of a higher order had the Irish harp drawn in gold leaf on a green ground, encircled with the words '*Erin ga braugh*!', signifying 'Ireland for ever!' Others, of a more desperate turn, had a broad green ribbon bound entirely round their hats, with 'Liberty and Equality' in large letters in the front.[30]

The rebels immediately began a noisy celebration of Ireland's version of the French Revolution. Some were soon drunk on whisky; a few, rashly and prematurely, were seen to light their pipes with pound notes to show the uselessness of government money. Wexford's citizens, whatever their real feelings, thought it politic to hang out green flags, or put pieces of green in their windows; some affixed to their doors hastily improvised posters proclaiming LIBERTY AND FRATERNITY.

Captains of the fishing-fleet in the harbour, who for inflated fees had taken on board Protestant families hoping to reach the safety of Wales, now returned their passengers to the quayside, where arrest and imprisonment awaited the males. Soon two hundred Protestants had been jailed by rebels for whom the terms 'Loyalist', 'Protestant', and 'Orangeman' were synonymous. Ironically, the insurgents on occupying Wexford had released a Protestant prisoner from the same jail, and, because of his social standing, made him their commander-in-chief.

Beauchamp Bagenal Harvey, of Bargay Castle, was a Protestant, a landowner, a magistrate – and a United Irishman. Dr Colclough and Edward Fitzgerald, Catholic gentry arrested on Saturday night with Harvey, became rebel colonels. Captain Matthew Keogh, a retired British Army officer, was made military governor. Saturday's arrests, it was said, had been made on information wrung by pitch-capping from a United Irishman named Perry.

There is an interesting mention of this group of radical gentry in the Personal Sketches *of Sir Jonah Barrington, the judge, who in April 1798 attended a dinner-party at Bargay Castle, when the table-talk convinced him that an insurrection was imminent.*

... that evening proved to me one of great uneasiness, and made a very disagreeable impression both on my mind and spirits. The company I met included Captain Keogh; the two unfortunate Counsellors Sheers, who were both hung shortly afterwards; Mr Colclough, who was hung on the bridge; Mr Hay, who was also executed; Mr William Hatton, one of the rebel directory of Wexford, who unaccountably escaped; and a gentleman of the bar whose name I shall not mention, as he still lives.

The entertainment was good, and the party cheerful. Temple freaks were talked over; the bottle circulated: but, at length, Irish politics became the topic, and proceeded to an extent of disclosure which utterly surprised me.... The probability of a speedy revolt was freely discussed, though in the most artful manner, not a word of any of the party committing themselves: but they talked it over as a result which might be expected from the complexion of the times and the irritation excited in consequence of the severities exercised by the government. The chances of success, in the event of a rising were openly debated, as were also the circumstances likely to spring from that success, and the examples which the insurgents would in such a case probably make. All this was at the same time talked over, without one word being uttered in favour of rebellion: – a system of caution which, I afterwards learned, was much practised for the purpose of gradually making proselytes without alarming them. I saw through it clearly, and here my presentiments came strong upon me. I found myself in the midst of absolute though unavowed conspirators. I perceived that the explosion was much nearer than the government expected; and I was startled at the decided manner in which my host and his friends spoke.

Under these circumstances, my alternative was evidently to quit the house or give a turn to the conversation. I therefore began to laugh at the subject, and ridicule it as quite visionary, observing jestingly to Keogh – 'Now, my dear Keogh, it is quite clear that you and I, in this famous rebellion, shall be on different sides of the question; and of course one or the other of us must necessarily be hanged at or before its termination – I upon a lamp-iron in Dublin, or you on the bridge of Wexford. Now, we'll make a bargain! – if we beat you, upon my honour I'll do all I can to save your neck; and if your folk beat us, you'll save me from the honour of the lamp-iron!

We shook hands on the bargain, which created much merriment, and gave the whole after-talk a cheerful character; and I returned to Wexford at twelve at night, with a most decided impression of the danger of the country, and a complete presentiment that either myself or Captain Keogh would never see the conclusion of that summer.

I immediately wrote to Mr Secretary Cooke, without mentioning names, place, or any particular source of knowledge; but simply to assure him that there was not a doubt that an insurrection would break out at a much earlier period than the government expected. I desired him to ask me no questions, but said that he might depend upon the fact; adding that a commanding force ought instantly to be sent down to garrison the town of Wexford. 'If the government,' said I, in conclusion, 'does not attend to my warning, it must take the consequences.' My warning was not attended to; but His Majesty's government soon found I was right. They lost Wexford, and might have lost Ireland, by that culpable inattention.[7]

It has been suggested (by R. R. Madden, for one) that Sir Jonah was asked some questions, and did give names. There is no evidence to support this.

In his new role of rebel Commander-in-Chief, Harvey enlisted the aid of the mayor of Wexford, Dr Jacob, and a few town notables to maintain order. All carpenters and blacksmiths were put to manufacturing pikes. Patrol boats went out from the harbour and seized several ships carrying provisions to Dublin. Lord Kingsborough arrived by boat into Wexford, expecting to join the North Cork militia, of which he was Colonel, but instead was seized by the rebels and thrust into the overcrowded jail. At great risk to their lives and property, some Catholics hid terrified Protestants. Dr Caulfield, the Catholic Bishop of Wexford, spent 'from morning to night ... writing, speaking, and pleading for them [*Protestants*] to procure protection from the chiefs of the insurrection'.[12]

For a short time Charles Jackson escaped capture:

About eight o'clock the next morning, May 31st, the old woman, who owned the cabin, came home, (she was a Roman Catholic), and I made myself known to her, begging in the most earnest manner that she would permit me to remain concealed there until affairs were a little settled. She told me she would as long as she could without endangering herself, and that she would go into town and see how matters went, which she accordingly did; and, in about two hours, returned with information that the insurgents were searching all the houses for Protestants, and committing them to jail; and further told me, if I should be found there, that they would kill her and burn the house, therefore it was necessary I should go to some other place. I thought it prudent to comply. She then gave me some bread and beer, and advised me to try and get among the fields, and lay in the hedges by day, and travel by night.

Accordingly, now, as every house was shut against me, and I had no friend to fly to for refuge, I got out at her back-door, and went about two miles across the country, when I met an old woman, and requested her to show me what road I had better take to effect my escape. She told me it was in vain to attempt it; for that, if I did not belong to the rebels, my own brother would betray me. I left her and went on, but soon heard voices behind me, calling on me to stop, and I should have mercy. I turned round, and saw six men advancing with pikes in their hands. They seized me, and conducted me back to town, and then put me into jail, in which I found about 220

Protestants. The jail is a very strong building, situated at a short distance from the barracks, and so built round with walls that you can see no person whatever pass or repass.

Towards evening, a fellow, of the name of Dick Monk, who had formerly been a shoe-black in the town, but now was raised by the rebels to the rank of a captain, came into the jail, and bid us prepare our souls for death, for that all of us, except such, as upon examination, he should release, would be put to death at twelve o'clock that night. The manner of his examining was two-fold. First, politically; and, then, religiously. The form of his political examination was this:

Quest. Are you straight?
Ans. I am.
Quest. How straight?
Ans. As straight as a rush.
Quest. Go on then.
Ans. In Truth, in Trust, in Unity, and in Liberty.
Quest. What have you got in your hand?
Ans. A green bough.
Quest. Where did it first grow?
Ans. In America.
Quest. Where did it bud?
Ans. In France.
Quest. Where are you going to plant it?
Ans. In the Crown of Great Britain.*

**Some other sources giving this catechism say 'In the Crown of Ireland.'*

They then gave each other the hand, but in a way I did not understand. The preceding questions and answers, however, appeared to be a part of the United Irishmen's catechism, by which they know each other.

The religious examination was this:

Quest. Are you a Christian? If the person answered Yes, he was required to bless himself, and say the Ave Maria. If he could do this, in the Roman Catholic manner, and go through the other form, then he was acquitted.[30]

Jackson was one of three prisoners selected to form a firing squad to execute a man named Murphy who had given evidence against some United Irishmen at the previous Assizes.

... the dead march was struck up, and beat from the jail to the place of execution, which was a mile and a half off, on the other side of the bridge, on a wide strand. The procession passed by my house. When I came opposite to it, I was so much affected as almost to faint: some water was brought me, and I proceeded. As soon as we reached the destined spot, all the rebels, with their arms in their hands, knelt down, and prayed for about five minutes. This I understood was because the victim was a Roman Catholic. An order was then given to form a half-circle, with an opening to the water. The poor man was directed to kneel down, with his back to the water, and his face towards us, which he did, with his hands clasped. I requested to be allowed to tie my cravat round his eyes. They told me not to be too nice about the matter; for, in a few minutes, it would be my own case. The muskets were then called for, but it was suggested, that if they gave us three muskets, we might turn and fire at them; on which it was settled that we should fire one at a time. The first appointed to fire was Mathews, and it was remarkable that the piece misfired three times. During this time the countenance of the condemned man exhibited such an appearance of inexpressible terror as shall never be effaced from my memory. The man who owned the musket was damned, and asked, 'What sort of piece was that to carry to a field of battle?' A common sporting-gun was then brought, and fired by Mathews, and the ball hit the poor man in the arm. I was next called upon ... I fired, and the poor man fell dead....[30]

Other executions followed; but the one man who may at that time have been able to prevent them was no longer in Wexford. Commander-in-Chief Harvey had taken a large part of the rebel army west with the aim of attacking the garrison at New Ross, by taking which he would cut off the supply route to the government's military base at Waterford. This was a key encounter; success for the rebels could have ignited the whole of the south in heady insurrection. Two other columns moved out from Wexford: one north-west to Bunclody [Newtownbarry] towards County Wicklow, one north-east to Gorey and Arklow and the road to Dublin.

The critical situation for the government was eased considerably by the outcome of the assault on New Ross. Yet it was a battle the rebels probably should have won, and in a day of fluctuating fortunes at times appeared to have won.

Bagenal Harvey pitched his camp at Corbet Hill, looking down on the town from the east. Part of the medieval fortifications had been broken up after the town's surrender to Cromwell, and the gates had been widened; but New Ross was an impressive sight to the rebel force, with its walls, its nine towers, and its five gates. General Henry Johnson commanded the garrison. Shortly before the rebels attacked, Lord Mountjoy – popular with Catholic troops for having proposed the first Catholic Relief Act (1778) – brought in a large contingent of his Dublin militia, increasing the garrison's strength to just over two thousand men. General Johnson stationed his forward men outside the Three Bullet Gate, to the east, and also the North or Bishop's Gate. Inside the town, the strongest concentration of forces was at the barracks, the jail, the market-place, the main-guard, and at the wooden bridge across the Barrow River on to which the town backed to the south. Mindful that the short swords of the cavalry had fared disastrously against the long pikes of the rebels in earlier engagements in the rebellion, the General wisely kept his mounted men in reserve on the quay at the back of the town.

Thomas Cloney, the young farmer who had been drawn reluctantly into armed conflict, of which he had no experience, was given command of 500 men at New Ross. From his account of the day's fighting, we can see that the courage of the majority of the rebels amd their considerable numerical superiority was offset by factors militating against success for the rebels at New Ross and throughout the country. Hundreds deserted before and during engagements. Most were inexperienced in the use of firearms, often committing the novice's fault of firing too high, and when they captured cannon, they either did not know how to fire them or fired innacurately (some blew up, killing their handlers). Due to a shortage of officers, the rebels kept close together and took their lead from what their neighbours were doing: thus a move forward tended to be a move forward of the whole army, and all retreated when one group did. Then too, the temptation to sample freely of stores of liquor *come across in the course of the fighting was too great for many to resist, and this could turn victory into sudden defeat.*

Thomas Cloney came across the bravery, as well as the inexperience and indiscipline, when he commanded at New Ross.

An aide-de-camp, Matthew Furlong, offered to carry a message from General Harvey to the Commander-in-Chief of the King's forces asking him to surrender the town of New Ross.

Sir, – As a friend to humanity, I request you will surrender the town of Ross to the Wexford forces now assembled. Your resistance will but provoke rapine and plunder, to the ruin of the most innocent. Flushed with victory, the Wexford forces, now innumerable and irresistible, will not be controlled if they meet with any resistance; to prevent, therefore, the total ruin of all property in the town, I urge you to a speedy surrender, which you will be forced to do in a few hours with loss and bloodshed, as you are surrounded on all sides. Your answer is required in four hours. Mr Furlong carries this letter and will bring the answer.

I am, Sir, etc. etc.

B. B. Harvey

Central camp at Corbet Hill,

Half-past 3 o'clock, Morning June 5, 1798.

He [*Mr Furlong*] advanced to the nearest out-post of the King's troops, without fear or trepidation, and on announcing his mission, his body was instantly perforated by the bullets of an inhuman soldiery....

Mr Furlong's fall rendered the people so furious, that they became almost unmanageable, and it was resolved to send the intrepid Colonel John Kelly forward with five hundred men, to drive in the out-posts of the King's troops, who had occupied the fields and ditches between our camp and the town ... Colonel Kelly had now advanced with five hundred men of his battalion of Bantry men, and I had orders, in case he was unable to drive back the out-posts, to advance with five hundred men of my battalion of Bantry men to support him. The men of the barony of Bantry, which is by far the largest in the county Wexford, were divided into two battalions, each consisting perhaps of about fifteen hundred men.... To such a young hero as Kelly, and with such men as he commanded, no daring was too great; he but too successfully performed his duty, for having drove his opponents in full flight before him, the enthusiasm of the main body could no longer be restrained; they all poured down in one and the same direction, without order or control. . . .

Lord Mountjoy, who had advanced in front of his regiment, the County Dublin Militia, to remonstrate with the people, fell by a rash hand, such as that which slew poor Furlong . . . The acts on both sides happened, however, without the sanction of persons in authority at either sides. Having advanced near the Three Bullet Gate, parties of the King's troops still retained their positions at both sides of the road, and we were exposed to a cross fire from both, while Colonel Kelly and his men were endeavouring to force an entrance into the town. On the right of the road several of my men were placed under cover of a very high ditch, from which they kept up a hot fire on those soldiers who were inside to the right of the gate, and in the rear, or on the walls of some burned cabins; one soldier particularly distinguished himself by standing to the last on a wall, in a very exposed situation, and firing at our men as they advanced. The heads of our party alone were exposed, and such was the coolness of the soldier, his intrepidity, and the correctness of his aim, that he actually scalped, in part, one man by my side, by his shot taking off the skin and hair from the top of his forehead. He also wounded a man at the other side by a shot, which took the skin off one of his temples. A person close to me, at length levelled at him and tumbled him by his shot, overhead and heels from his post into the still smoking thatch of the burning cabin on whose wall he had stood. . . .

In about half-an-hour the King's troops were dislodged from the fields, and after an obstinate resistance, driven back from the Gate . . .

Colonel Kelly now advanced to the Barracks, not very far distant from the Gate, where he received a shot in one of his thighs, which disabled him, and deprived us of his services. . . . The Barrack was, however, soon taken, and arms and ammunition obtained, which had been deposited there. . . .

While we were thus engaged, a strong body of cavalry came from the town by a lane in our rear, for the purpose of charging our detached wing. Many of our men who were retreating, returned, and we, who were between this party of our men and the Gate, faced about, and as the cavalry were thus placed between the muskets and pikes of both detachments, Cornet Dodwell and twenty-eight of the 5th Dragoons were slain in a few minutes, the business being done almost exclusively by our pikesmen. The fallen Dragoons were hastily stripped of their arms by a famous Amazon among us, whose name was Doyle, and whom we called 'the point of war' . . .

We now entered the town in triumph, and the main body of General Johnson's army, after a resistance not so formidable as might have been expected from beloved champions of the Irish Ascendancy, fled before us over the bridge into the county of Kilkenny . . .

After being some time in the town, and finding our men entering houses, to seek for liquor and refreshment, we found it prudent to retire to the Three Bullet Gate, lest the main body of the King's troops might return and take advantage of our confusion. When we had remained some time at the Gate, we mustered as good a force as possible and entered the town again, by what is called the Broguemakers' Lane, which leads down nearly on a line with the church. To this spot we brought down one of the howitzers, taken at the Three Rocks, with which to fire on the main guard, but on going down some distance beyond the church, we were so warmly fired on from the houses, that we were obliged to retreat, after sending in vain to the Three Bullet Gate, to General Harvey for a reinforcement, which he was not able to supply.

It is evident that our commanders and the King's officers were equally ignorant of the disposition or strength of the respective armies. There was no reconnoitring, no changes of position, or great military skill displayed at either side, but two confused masses of men, struggling alternately to drive the other back by force alone.

Having fallen back to the Three Bullet Gate, it was quite disheartening to behold the smallness of our numbers, yet the few who remained seemed to prefer death to the abandonment of a victory, which, throughout the day, appeared to be within their grasp. It is

1. Portrait of Oliver Cromwell by Lely

2. William of Orange, the Protestant hero, receives idealized depiction on banners carried in traditional Orange parades in Northern Ireland. His crossing of the Boyne is the most favoured motif

3. The Death of Schomberg (at the Battle of the Boyne) by Jan Wyck

4. Wolfe Tone

5. Prior to the 1798 rising rebel suspects were sometimes subjected to torture by pitch-capping. Pitch mixed with gunpowder was pressed over the victim's skull and set alight. Captain Swayne, here depicted, was killed in the rebellion

6. Henry Joy McCracken, by Miss S. C. Harrison

7. Henry Joy McCracken's National Volunteer uniform

8. James Hope

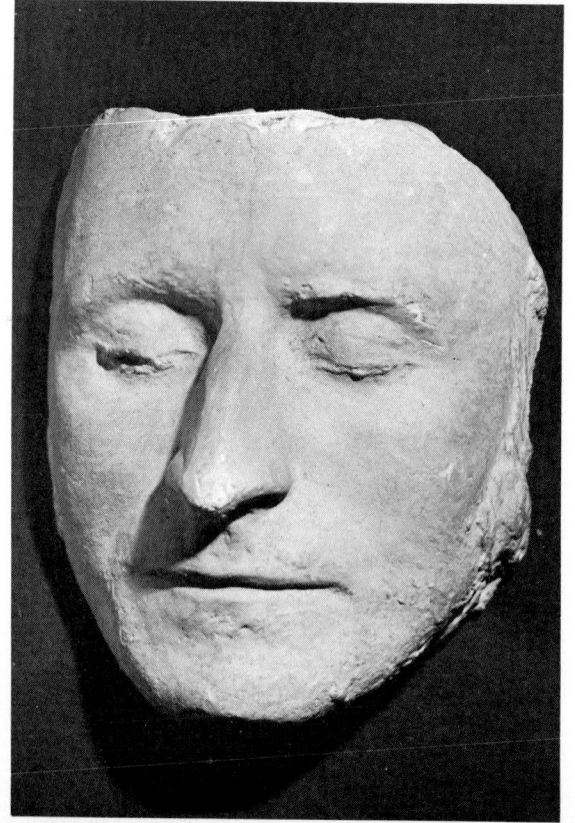

9. The Battle of Ballynahinch by Thomas Robinson

10. Death mask of Wolfe Tone

11. Robert Emmet

12. William Smith O'Brien

13. Thomas Francis Meagher

14. Charles Gavan Duffy

right:

15. 8 May 1915. March past in Belfast of the 36th (Ulster) Division, formed out of the Ulster Volunteer Force, who had armed to oppose Home Rule. They suffered terrible casualties at the Somme

16. General Sir George Richardson and Sir Edward Carson (wearing Homburg hat and dark overcoat) on their way to review 36th (Ulster) Division at Malone, Belfast, 8 May 1915

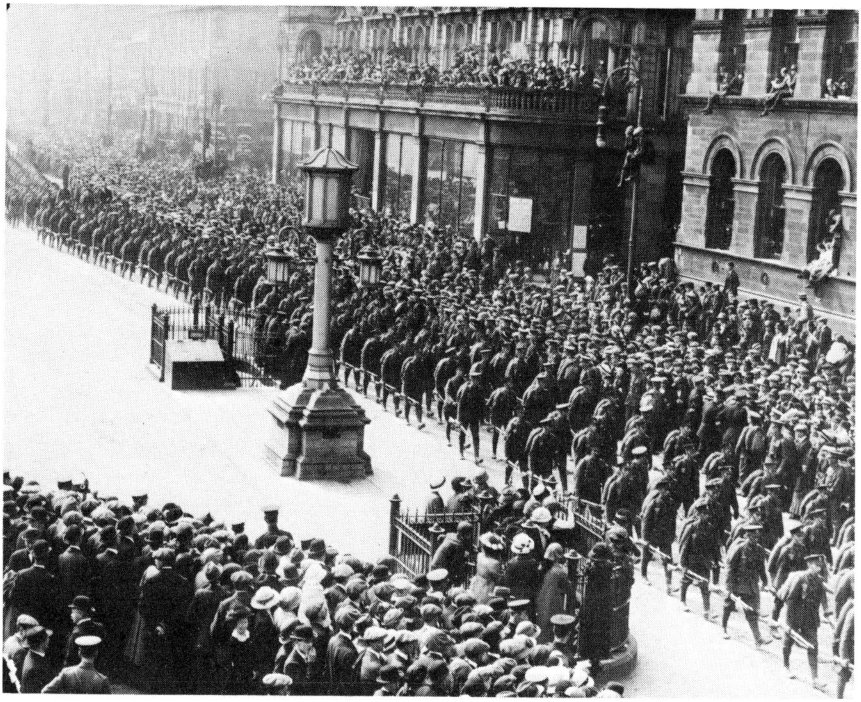

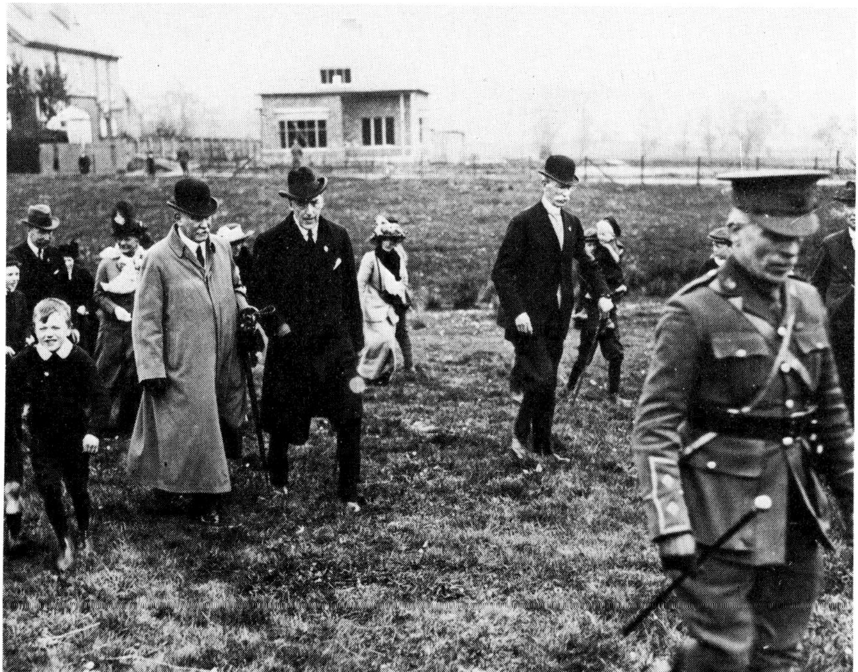

Ulster's Solemn League and Covenant.

Being convinced in our consciences that Home Rule would be disastrous to the material well-being of Ulster as well as of the whole of Ireland, subversive of our civil and religious freedom, destructive of our citizenship and perilous to the unity of the Empire, we, whose names are underwritten, men of Ulster, loyal subjects of His Gracious Majesty King George V., humbly relying on the God whom our fathers in days of stress and trial confidently trusted, do hereby pledge ourselves in solemn Covenant throughout this our time of threatened calamity to stand by one another in defending for ourselves and our children our cherished position of equal citizenship in the United Kingdom and in using all means which may be found necessary to defeat the present conspiracy to set up a Home Rule Parliament in Ireland. And in the event of such a Parliament being forced upon us we further solemnly and mutually pledge ourselves to refuse to recognise its authority. In sure confidence that God will defend the right we hereto subscribe our names. And further, we individually declare that we have not already signed this Covenant.

The above was signed by me at _____
"Ulster Day," Saturday, 28th September, 1912.

God Save the King.

17. Ulster's Solemn League and Covenant

POBLACHT NA H EIREANN.
THE PROVISIONAL GOVERNMENT
OF THE
IRISH REPUBLIC
TO THE PEOPLE OF IRELAND.

IRISHMEN AND IRISHWOMEN: In the name of God and of the dead generations from which she receives her old tradition of nationhood, Ireland, through us, summons her children to her flag and strikes for her freedom.

Having organised and trained her manhood through her secret revolutionary organisation, the Irish Republican Brotherhood, and through her open military organisations, the Irish Volunteers and the Irish Citizen Army, having patiently perfected her discipline, having resolutely waited for the right moment to reveal itself, she now seizes that moment, and, supported by her exiled children in America and by gallant allies in Europe, but relying in the first on her own strength, she strikes in full confidence of victory.

We declare the right of the people of Ireland to the ownership of Ireland, and to the unfettered control of Irish destinies, to be sovereign and indefeasible. The long usurpation of that right by a foreign people and government has not extinguished the right, nor can it ever be extinguished except by the destruction of the Irish people. In every generation the Irish people have asserted their right to national freedom and sovereignty; six times during the past three hundred years they have asserted it in arms. Standing on that fundamental right and again asserting it in arms in the face of the world, we hereby proclaim the Irish Republic as a Sovereign Independent State, and we pledge our lives and the lives of our comrades-in-arms to the cause of its freedom, of its welfare, and of its exaltation among the nations.

The Irish Republic is entitled to, and hereby claims, the allegiance of every Irishman and Irishwoman. The Republic guarantees religious and civil liberty, equal rights and equal opportunities to all its citizens, and declares its resolve to pursue the happiness and prosperity of the whole nation and of all its parts, cherishing all the children of the nation equally, and oblivious of the differences carefully fostered by an alien government, which have divided a minority from the majority in the past.

Until our arms have brought the opportune moment for the establishment of a permanent National Government, representative of the whole people of Ireland and elected by the suffrages of all her men and women, the Provisional Government, hereby constituted, will administer the civil and military affairs of the Republic in trust for the people.

We place the cause of the Irish Republic under the protection of the Most High God, Whose blessing we invoke upon our arms, and we pray that no one who serves that cause will dishonour it by cowardice, inhumanity, or rapine. In this supreme hour the Irish nation must, by its valour and discipline and by the readiness of its children to sacrifice themselves for the common good, prove itself worthy of the august destiny to which it is called.

Signed on behalf of the Provisional Government,
THOMAS J. CLARKE.
SEAN Mac DIARMADA,   THOMAS MacDONAGH,
P. H. PEARSE,   EAMONN CEANNT,
JAM. CONNOLLY.   JOSEPH PLUNKETT.

18. Proclamation of the Republic

19. James Connolly

right:

20. A British machine gun section in the South Dublin area, April 1916

21. Rebels take position behind a barricade, Dublin 1916

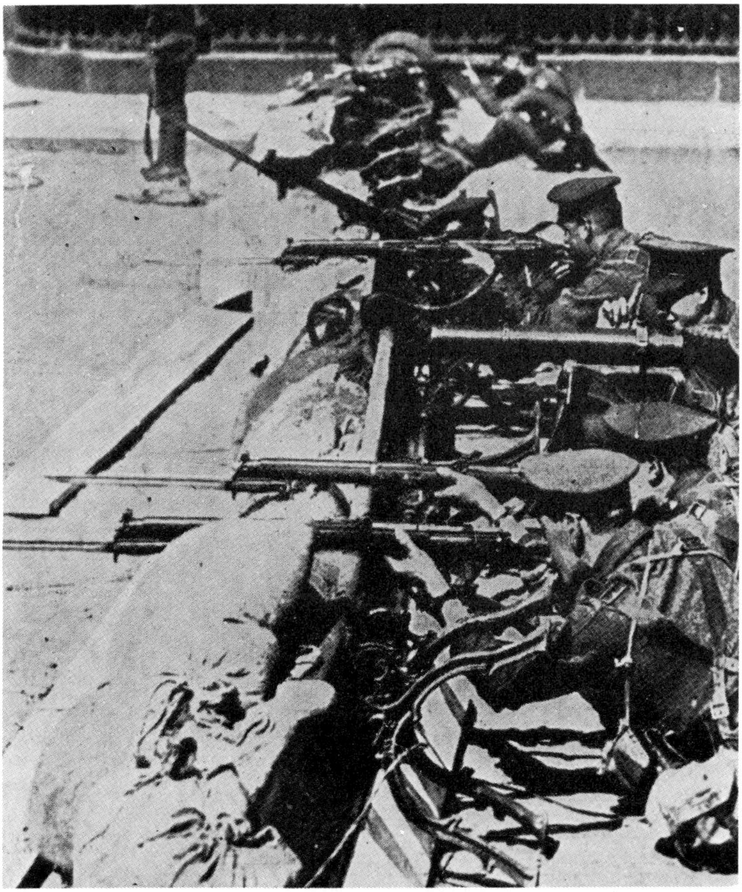

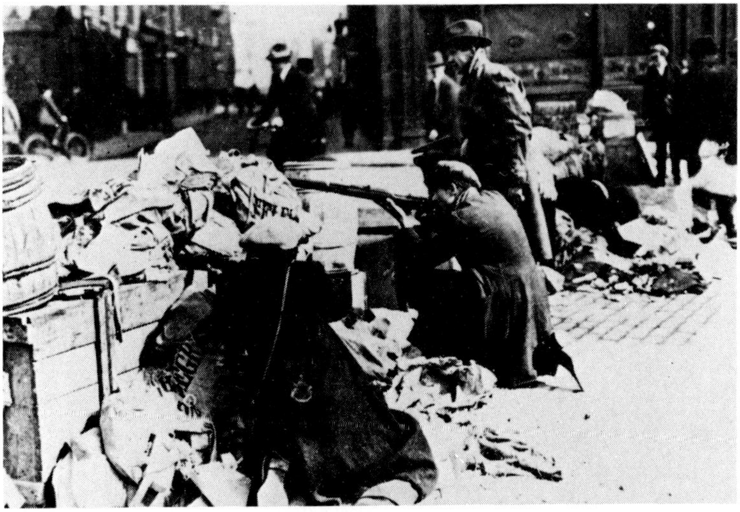

22. The burned out G.P.O. in Dublin attracted thousands of sightseers

23. Rebel prisoners being marched out of Dublin, May 1916

24. (Left of picture) Count Plunkett's three sons—Joseph, George, and John, after surrender. Joseph was shot. George and John had their death sentences commuted to ten years' penal servitude

25. Britain's Irish problem persists. Troops face I.R.A. bombers and snipers in Belfast 1969

26. The blazing British Embassy in Dublin, 2 February 1972, fired in violent protest against the 'Bloody Sunday' shootings in Londonderry.
Courtesy Syndication International

almost incredible with what indifference, nay, even cheerfulness, many of the peasantry exhibited their bleeding wounds, declaring they felt pride in having it known that they bled in the cause of Ireland. Several whose wounds were mortal, only inquiring in their last moments, 'was victory on our side', and being answered in the affirmative, they said then, 'they died happy'. I proposed to General Harvey that we should send a kind of forlorn hope through some open fields, called *beurheena slanaigh*, to attack the Clare Militia, in the Irishtown, but we could not muster above forty men for that purpose.

As we advanced through a gateway, leading up to the fields before mentioned, a religious enthusiast was placed on his knees in the passage, holding a crucifix in his hands, and pressing every man as he passed him to kneel down and kiss it. Some men who advanced before me complied, although they were exposed to a very hot fire. I was not, however, anxious to make any delay in such a warm spot, as my faith was not, as I believe, so strong as that of this devotee. It is, however, an extraordinary fact, that he remained a considerable time in this dangerous position unhurt and unappalled. Our party advanced rapidly through the first field, but when I arrived at the ditch that separated us from the main body, I could not get a man to ascend it, so that we had to retreat with greater precipitation than we advanced, exposed to a most galling fire, by which numbers of our men were either killed or wounded. Here the contest ended, after about thirteen hours almost constant fighting, with considerable loss on both sides.

The garrison, which consisted of about two thousand men, of all arms, with several pieces of cannon, were opposed by not much more than three thousand of our men, who were engaged after the first two hours in the morning. The loss on either side never could be accurately ascertained, but was supposed to have been about three hundred killed on each side, and about five hundred on each side wounded....

I foresaw the calamities that were likely to follow our failure, and I would rather have fallen on the field that day than to retire from it defeated. The persecution that we were destined to suffer might easily be conceived, when we recollected what we had experienced before any hostile movement was made against the army.[13]

The following account by one of the defenders, an artillery officer, describes an extraordinary incident in the fighting when one of the rebels decided on an unconventional method of silencing a cannon.

The rebels advanced, driving before them all the black cattle they could collect through the country, to disorder our ranks; which was in some measure prevented, by a few discharges of grapeshot. The action was commenced by the fourth flank battalion; indeed such a close well-directed fire I never before saw. I was an idle spectator for upwards of two hours and a half. At near seven o'clock, the army began to retreat in all directions. I had the honour to command a six-pounder fieldpiece. The rebels pouring in like a flood, artillery was called for, and human blood began to flow down the street. Though hundreds were blown to pieces by our grapeshot, yet thousands behind them, being intoxicated from drinking during the night, and void of fear, rushed upon us. The cavalry were now ordered to make a charge through them, when a terrible carnage ensued: they were cut down like grass; but the pikemen being called to the front, and our swords being too short to reach them, obliged the horse to retreat, which put us in some confusion. We kept up the action till about half-past eight; and it was maintained with such obstinacy on both sides, that it was doubtful who would keep the field. They then began to burn and destroy the town – it was on fire in many places in about fifteen minutes. By this time the insurgents advanced as far as the main-guard, where there was a most bloody conflict; but with the assistance of two ship-guns placed in the street, we killed a great number of them, and beat them back for some time. The Dublin County regiment, headed by their colonel, Lord Mountjoy, now made another attack on the rebels, and the action being revived in all quarters of the town with double fury, many heroes fell, and among them the brave Mountjoy: this so exasperated his regiment, that they fought like furies, and now indeed was the scene truly bloody. Our forces for the third time being overpowered by the weight of such a body pouring down upon us, we retreated beyond the bridge, when General Johnson came galloping up, crying, 'Soldiers, I will lay my bones this day in Ross, will you let me lie alone?'

Major Vesey, of the Dublin County, the next in command to Lord Mountjoy, again led his men over the bridge, exhorting them to revenge for the loss of their colonel. The whole brigade (except some who fled to Waterford) being led on by General Johnson – as brave a commander as ever drew sword – were determined to retake the town, to conquer or to die. Again we opened a tremendous fire on the rebels, which was as fiercely returned. We retook the cannon which had been taken from the King's forces in a former engagement, and turned them on the enemy. The gun I had the honour to command being called to the main-guard, shocking was it to see the dreadful carnage that was there; it continued for half an hour obstinate and bloody: the thundering of cannon shook the town, the very windows were shivered in pieces with the dreadful concussion. I believe six hundred rebels lay dead in the Main Street; they would often come within a few yards of the guns. One fellow ran up, and taking off his hat and wig, thrust them up the cannon's mouth the length of his arm, calling to the rest, 'Blood-an'-'ounds, my boys, come take her now, she's stopt, she's stopt!'

The action was doubtful and bloody from four in the morning to four in the evening, when they began to give way in all quarters, and shortly after fled in every direction; leaving behind them all their cannon, baggage, provisions, and several hogsheads of wine, whisky, brandy, etc. which we spilled, lest they should have been poisoned. It was past five before we finally routed them....[4]

Our third, and last, eye-witness at New Ross was a schoolteacher resident in the town. General Johnson had disarmed the uniformless civilian volunteers shortly before the battle commenced, but James Alexander, who had fought in the royal army in America against the colonists, was determined to see what was happening in the streets, even though his life was recurrently in danger from the soldiers of both armies engaged.

As I approached near the main-guard, which was stationed at the Court House in this street, some of the remoter soldiers called to the rest, 'Shoot that fellow! Stick him!' I laughingly exclaimed, 'Ye bloody backs!' Upon this two men levelled at, and no doubt would have shot me, but for the interference of some of my last evening's guard, who mentioned the General's friendship for me, as though it were particular. I passed by and was going further up the street, when my good friends called me back; but the rest bid me, 'Go on and fear nothing', expecting as I was afterwards told, *that I should be shot*! Still I advanced up the street, but not halfway when I heard a close bustle of I knew not what, as the street was so incurvated that I could not see. All this time a remote firing went on, but not without some intermission, which space was filled with huzzas. I advanced now but slowly, straining myself to see as far up the street as possible, without the hazards of advancing too far. Presently I heard a hasty muttering of about twenty voices and a rattling which I naturally and justly conjectured to be cannon wheels. Five or six muskets now went off. They were succeeded by two, then by about four; then about a dozen; and at last by a heavy shower for about one minute. This was at the Church Lane. At last a piece of ordnance went off, which was followed by a fearful shout of one party and a triumphant huzza of another. I was still on the gape, and making long strides. A very loose firing of musketry now began again, and a party of rebels appeared stalking down the street, in attitudes not unlike my own. I turned about in order to alarm the guard; but lo! – a strong body of the King's troops with *Grumbling Bess* – a roaring nine-pounder stopped up the lower part of the street, not quite so high as the shambles; and the rebels made a stand just above the belly of the curve; so that one party could hardly see the other. In this extremity what could I do? I got close up against a shop door exactly facing Bakehouse Lane. . . . On each side of me were bow windows, by which I was completely concealed from both parties. Now a dreadful pause took place, neither rebels nor soldiers fully appearing to each other. I popped out my head, and asked the rebels if I might pass through them? But an old, strong, well-made man, in a very wretched trim 'ifted up his clumsy withered claw and shook it at me exclaiming, 'Fon! Fon! Fon!' I took his advice and kept close. Meantime the soldiers advanced in front of their cannon. The rebels also began to show themselves. A few musket shots were exchanged on both sides. Two rebels dropped, and one was wounded, and began to howl like a *Chickasaw Indian* when he hears the war-whoop. But very few of the shots on either side were fired with proper judgment. Most of them owing to the cowardly positions of some, struck against the walls of the hollow side of the street. I now observed an important circumstance, which I hoped to tell the mainguard: the rebels balls flew (comparatively speaking) amazingly feeble. Hence it was evident that their powder was wretchedly inferior to that of our troops. I have been told since that it was manufactured for them at Wexford.... Still a shy firing was kept on, without any further effect; but at last both parties as if by mutual consent appeared full in each other's view.... Both parties began a clumsy sort of fire, when, suddenly the soldiers opening their cannon upon them, blew numbers of them off their legs; amongst whom was my friend Mr 'Fon! Fon!'[3]

After coming close in several incidents to being killed by the royal troops, Alexander was finally persuaded to retire to the comparative safety of his house.

Exactly at half an hour after two, some of my brave and humane friends in tribulation called on me, and told me, that *the battle was now too remote to affect the town; that, for their parts, they were too much fatigued in the late desperate charge to follow on; but that, if I chose I might now come under their protection and see the town and the slain.* I did so, and saw the streets literally strewed with dead carcases. The greatest slaughter was in the Main Street, especially near the churchyard. The piece of cannon planted on an eminence just above the Church Lane did very much the greatest execution than any other. Next to the Main Street, the greatest slaughter was around the town wall, where the battle raged. Next, the Chapel Lane, 'twas horrible. Next, Broguemaker's Lane, Michael Street, and the Cross Lane; in all which lanes the number of slain on the same length of ground was pretty equal; with this exception that, in the Broguemaker's Lane many were burned to ashes ... Amongst the slain in the Main Street I saw bodies with frightful wounds of about one fortnight's standing, evidently distinguishable from those received on this day. It is almost incredible that men with such large, deep, raw wounds could bear the fatigue even of the march from Wexford or Enniscorthy. Some of those gashes were nearly, if not entirely, to the bone, and six inches long! . . . The rebel carcases lay in the streets unburied for three or four days, some perforated over and over with musket balls, or the bayonet; some hacked with swords; some mangled and torn with grapeshot, and still worse, with *pigs*, some of which I have seen eating the brains out of cloven skulls and gnawing the flesh about the raw wounds! Many rebels were reduced to ashes; many burned to a cinder; and, many partly burned, and partly roasted, till their flesh looked like roast pork. Amongst the slain were also many dead pigs.[3]

Meanwhile there occurred that day at Scullabogue one of the two unforgettable atrocities of the rebellion in Wexford. As the battle was raging at New Ross, rumours of defeat and slaughter of the rebels was circulating at Scullabogue House, belonging to a gentleman called Captain King, where upwards of two hundred prisoners, mostly Protestants, were being held. An order was given, it is not sure by whom, that the prisoners should be killed. Thirty-five were shot on the lawn. The others, including women and children, were burned alive in a barn when guards set fire to the thatch: the charred bodies remained standing upright in the confined space.

Bagenal Harvey, horrified and sickened by the massacre at Scullabogue, at once issued an edict . . . any person or persons who shall take upon him or them to kill or murder any person or prisoner, burn any house, or commit any plunder, without any special written orders from the commander-in-chief, shall suffer death."[25] *It was his last order as military commander-in-chief, for he was deposed and command given to Father Philip Roche. Harvey returned to Wexford, where with precarious authority he attempted to control civic affairs. To a fellow Protestant who asked for 'protection', Harvey wrote:*

I from my heart wish to protect all property; I can scarce protect myself. . . . I took my present situation in hopes of doing good and preventing mischief and had my advice been taken by those in power the present mischief would never have arisen. . . . God knows where the business will end, but end how it will the good men of both parties will inevitably be ruined.[25]

The second great atrocity took place on the bridge at Wexford. But before returning to events at Wexford, we look briefly at the fates of the two rebel columns who had moved north.

The Bunclody (Newtownbarry) column was commanded by a giant priest, Father Kearns. His great weight had saved his life during the French Terror: hung from a lamp-post, the iron bent until his toes rested on the pavement. The rebel force he led forced the King's militia from Bunclody, but so many got drunk on looted liquor that the Crown troops easily recaptured the town.

The third rebel column defeated government troops at Tuberneering, then attacked the key town of Arklow on 9 June. If Arklow fell, only the garrison at Wicklow stood between the insurgents and an attack on Dublin itself. Our participant witness is Archibald MacLaren, serving with a Highland regiment . . .

. . . ordered out about a quarter of a mile to line the ditches on each side of the main road where the enemy was advancing. When the Croppies appeared with their green flags fixed to pole-heads in imitation of colours; they fired, which compliment was returned. As I did not think my Halbert a proper weapon to annoy the enemy at a distance, I exchanged it for a firelock. . . . I remember to have seen one fellow who stood in the centre of the road, neither advancing nor retreating, but seemingly encouraging others; several shots were fired at him without effect; but at length he was brought to the ground. When we had exchanged about a dozen rounds, and aide-de-camp from the General ordered us to retreat and join the Armagh in the street. This we did in seeming confusion, and the rebels, (no doubt), thinking that we fled, came on with great vaunting, setting up a loud huzza. One fellow, an officer, inspired with spirits and whisky (of which they had drank very copiously at a village called Collgreene), galloped in front, having something resembling a stand of colours in his hand . . . and waving his hat, called out 'Blood and wounds my boys! Come on, the town is ours!' But ere the foolhardy hero was aware, he turned the corner of a house which brought him almost to the mouth of a field-piece, surrounded by some hundreds of soldiers ready to fire or receive him on the points of their bayonets. . . . A volley of small shot laid his horse sprawling in the dust and broke his own thigh; though he fell under his horse he had cunning enough to lie still and might probably have passed for a dead man had he not . . . raised his head to take a peep round about him: this being observed four or five bayonets were plunged into his body. In the midst of his agony he stretched out his arm to shake hands with one of the soldiers. . . . But the soldier sent a bullet through his head. . . .[31]

The Highlander witnessed the last moments of Father Michael Murphy.
As he rode forward encouraging his troops to advance an unmannerly grapeshot obtruded itself upon his skull before the good man had time to put forth his hand to stop it. Some of his followers who saw him fall dragged him into a house. . . . Our troops to deprive them of their skulking places, set fire to one hut; the flames communicated with others and reached that in which the remains of the mob-deceiving Father Murphy lay. . . .

Two field pieces taken from the Londonderry at Gorey were played upon us from an eminence opposite the Durham and Cavan: but as the chief management of these pieces was entrusted to a sergeant of the Antrim who had been made their prisoner, we sustained no damage for some time, for at every shot he pointed with so much elevation that the balls whistled over our heads; but being observed by one of his officers, he was so far obliged to rectify this seeming mistake that the very next shot struck one of the Durham field pieces and smashed the carriage to pieces, which pleased the croppy officer so well that he cried out 'A hundred pounds for a soldier!' meaning I suppose that one trained soldier was better than many of his rude followers.

As the General was riding up street a man of seeming respectability came and told him that the rebels were making full speed for a lane which led (on the right of the barracks) from the river to the centre of the town. To check their progress the General ordered out a subaltern-sergeant and twelve men . . . As we turned down the lane to take possession of our post, we observed some hundreds of the united gentry advancing towards us; but we sent so many leaden messengers to forbid their visit, that many of them (to speak in a military style) fell back. . . . in a few minutes thereafter I was ordered up the street to observe how matters went on. As I passed through the lane an old woman popped her head out of a cabin door. 'Holy Jesus', said she, 'the sound of the guns shakes the cabin. . . .' By the time the sun was almost set, the rebels began to retreat in every direction. . . . As I was returning to the barrack my nose was accosted with a disagreeable smell. Upon enquiry I found it to proceed from the body of Father Murphy, whose leg and thigh were burnt into the very bone. . . . I could eat no more meat for some days. His head was fixed upon the wall of a burnt cabin. . . .[31]

In the view of the historian W.E.H. Lecky: 'The battle of Arklow was the last in which the rebels had any real chance of success, and from this time the rebellion rapidly declined.'

But at Wexford Charles Jackson and the other loyalist prisoners faced a horrible execution.

On Wednesday, June 20, about eight o'clock in the morning, we heard the drums beat to arms and the town bell ring, which was a sure sign to us of our friends being near; but, at the same time, we expected we should be cut off before they could arrive and release us. In this terrible state of suspense we remained till four o'clock in the afternoon, when we heard a horrid noise at the gate, and a demand of the prisoners. Eighteen or twenty were immediately taken out, and, in about half an hour, the rebels returned for more victims. In the whole, they took out ninety-eight. Those who were the last called out were seventeen in number. Mr Daniels and Mr Robinson, both gaugers; Mr Atkins, a tide-waiter; Mathews and Gourley, who were with me at the execution of Murphy; and myself; were included in this lot. The moment Mathews put his head out of the jail, he was shot dead; which, I believe, would have been the fate of us all, had not a Mrs Dickson (wife to a man who kept a public house in the town, and who had been made a captain by the rebels), when Mathews fell, immediately advanced, and desired they should desist, as they ought to allow the people on the bridge *the pleasure of seeing us*. We were accordingly marched to the bridge; and, when we came in sight of the people assembled there to witness the executions, they almost rent the air with shouts and exultations. I and my sixteen fellow-prisoners knelt down in a row. The blood of those who had been already executed on this spot (eighty-one in number) had more than stained, it streamed upon the ground about us. They first began the bloody tragedy by taking out Mr Daniels, who, the moment he was touched by their pikes, sprung over the battlements of the bridge into the water, where he was instantly shot. Mr Robinson was the next: he was piked to death. The manner of piking was by two of the rebels pushing their pikes into the front of the victim, while two others pushed pikes into his back, and in this state (writhing with torture) he was suspended aloft on the pikes till dead. He was then thrown over the bridge into the water. They ripped open the belly of poor Mr Atkins, and, in that condition, he ran several yards; when, falling on the side of the bridge, he was piked. Thus they proceeded till they came to Gourly, who was next to me. At that moment, one of them came up to me and asked me if I would have a priest. I felt my death to be certain, and I answered, 'No.' He then pulled me by the collar; but was desired to wait till Gourly was finished. While they were torturing him, General Roche rode up in great haste and bid them beat to arms; informing them that Vinegar Hill camp was beset and that reinforcements were wanting. This operated like lightning upon them: they all instantly quitted the bridge, and left Mr O'Connor, an organist, William Hamilton, the bailiff of the town, and myself on our knees. The mob (consisting of more women than men), which had been spectators of this dreadful scene, also instantly dispersed in every direction, supposing the King's troops were at hand. We were so stupefied by terror that we remained for some time in this posture without making the least effort to escape. The rebel-guard soon came to us, and took us back to the jail . . .[30]

The rebels' final stand in Wexford was at their main camp at Vinegar Hill, near Enniscorthy, on 21 June. The green flag that had flown for four weeks from the old windmill on the top of the hill was about to be hauled down, signifying the beginning of the end for the Republic. Following the turning of the tide for the government through the repulsions at New Ross and Arklow, General Gerard Lake, Commander-in-Chief, ordered a counter-attack by an army of more than ten thousand men that would drive the rebels towards Enniscorthy, on which five columns would converge. After taking Enniscorthy, Wexford would then be liberated. Lake himself came from Dublin to take command of the operation. The rebel camp on Vinegar Hill was encircled at all but one point, where General Francis Needham had not yet come into position; but four of Lake's five columns were ready to punish the republicans. Twenty thousand rebels packed together on the hill with inadequate protection presented a sitting target for cannons and howitzers. General Henry Johnson cleared the town of Enniscorthy in fierce street-fighting that cost him twenty dead, including two militia colonels, Lord Blayney and Colonel Vesey. After an hour's fighting, the surviving rebels fled in confusion through the one escape route open to them: the gap left by General Needham's late arrival.

Miles Byrne was one of the rebels defending Vinegar Hill:

At break of day the different corps began to quit their bivouacs, each to repair to the position assigned to them on the hill and on all the roads leading into the town of Enniscorthy. Our wounded men that we had transported on cars with us from the county of Wicklow, in order to have them placed in the hospital, we left at Drumgold, one of the suburbs of the town under Vinegar Hill; we had also to leave there a vast number of women and young girls who had followed their husbands and brothers, to escape from the English monsters who were devastating their homes. . . . Skirmishing at all our advanced posts commenced with the day; however the battle did not become general on the whole line before seven o'clock, but at daybreak several cannon shots were heard in different directions from the enemy's camps. These were signal guns, which proved to us that we were now nearly surrounded on all sides, except the Wexford one . . . I had not seen Vinegar Hill since the morning after the battle of Newtownbarry, the 2nd of June, and I was surprised to find that scarcely anything had been done to make it formidable against the enemy; the vast fences and ditches which surrounded it on three sides, and which should have been levelled to the ground, for at least a cannon shot, or half a mile's distance, were all untouched. The English forces, availing themselves of these fences, advanced from field to field, bringing with them their cannon, which they placed to great advantage behind and under the cover of the hedges and fences; whilst our men were exposed to a terrible fire from their artillery and small arms, without being able to drive them back from their strongholds in those fields.

Several columns of our pikemen however were instantly brought to attack the enemy's formidable position behind the fences in the fields, and it was in leading one of those desperate charges, that the splendid Dan Kervin was killed, at the head of the brave county Wicklow men. His death at this point was a severe loss, though he was soon replaced by a leader equally brave; yet his men could not be easily roused from the gloom cast over them by this misfortune; besides many fine fellows their comrades fell at the same moment beside Kervin. Indeed it is a miracle how the other chiefs escaped; that all displayed the greatest coolness and courage, charging at the head of their men under the tremendous fire of the enemy's batteries, which were sending cannon ball, grape shot, musket ball, as thickly as a shower of hail-stone....

I had been in many combats and battles, but I never before witnessed such a display of bravery and intrepidity as was shown all along our line, for nearly two hours, until our ammunition was expended. It was then recommended by some of our chiefs to assemble all our forces and attack the enemy's left flank, overturn it and march back to the county of Wicklow. At the commencement of the battle this plan might have been easily executed; but would it not have been cruel, and shameful, to abandon the town and the brave fellows who were defending it so heroically, and also to abandon our wounded men and the unfortunate families who had escaped and followed our camp?...

We afterwards effected our retreat tolerably well to the town of Wexford. And here our two armies that had separated on the 31st of May at the Windmill Hill near the town, then flushed with victory, one to go northwards to attack Gorey and Arklow, the other to go to take New Ross, met again, but unfortunately under very different circumstances, they being now completely dismayed and disheartened after our recent defeats; and it is grievous to think that our generals did not seem to have any preconcerted plan of action in face of the disasters as we were now experiencing.[11]

The relief of Wexford fell to General John Moore, later to become a British popular hero in the Peninsula campaign. He had brought a force up from Cork, and left New Ross the morning before the massacre by piking on Wexford Bridge. Moore's column did not consist of his regulars, but of inexperienced Irish militia, and with a less able general might have been defeated by a more numerous enemy when engaged at Foulk's Mill, about halfway between New Ross and Wexford. Moore himself led the charges.

My orders were to proceed that day to Taghmon, seven miles from Wexford. I waited till 3 p.m. for the troops that were to join me. Hearing then nothing of them, I determined to move forward. I had one thousand men under me; I thought this sufficient to hold my ground against the rebels; and as part of the general plan was for me to be at Taghmon that day I did not wish to disappoint it by failure on my side. I set out at 3 p.m. We had not marched above a mile when a cloud of dust was seen moving towards us. This we immediately perceived to be a large party of rebels. I knew something of the ground from having reconnoitred it in the morning. I immediately ordered the Yagers to advance and skirmish, whilst I formed part of the Light Infantry on the right and left of the road, and then ran forward the guns to a commanding situation at the crossing of two roads.

The attack began. The companies of Light Infantry, being unaccustomed to fire, hesitated a little. I was obliged to get off my horse to put myself at their head, to jump over a high ditch and advance on the enemy; we drove them downhill over a bridge. I directed Colonel Wilkinson to post himself at this bridge and prevent their passing it again. I ordered Major Aylmer with three companies of Light Infantry to march against a large body which were seen going round upon my left. He sent me word that they were in a wood near him, and seemed in such numbers that he was afraid to advance on them. I then sent them two more companies under Major Daniel and a field-piece, with directions to advance and ascertain the force of the enemy; to be cautious at first, but to follow them briskly if they staggered in the least. I was afraid to go from the front, opposite to which the enemy were in great numbers, and where I thought they were waiting for a favourable moment to fall upon me. The fire grew hotter upon the left, and messages for reinforcements were continually coming. I ordered the brigade major, Anderson, to go and let me know the true state of the left. He returned, and told me that it was absolutely necessary for me to go to the left immediately. I set off at a gallop, desiring him to stay and watch the movements at the front. I met the Light Infantry, the Yagers, and some Dragoons all in the woods mixed and retreating. The enemy was following close, and firing. I succeeded in stopping some immediately, and got them to jump out of the road and make a front on each side of it. I then encouraged the rest at first to halt, then to advance, and, when I saw them ready for it, I took off my hat, put my horse into a trot, gave a huzza, and got them to make a push. The tide immediately turned; we drove the rebels before us, and killed a great many.[33]

Moore ignored Lake's instructions to halt at Taghmon, seven miles from Wexford. He had received word that the lives of two hundred loyalist prisoners held in the town were in great danger, and risked marching on. Twelve yeomen with relatives in Wexford galloped ahead. That Moore's decision saved prisoners' lives was shown by what Mrs Brownrigg observed from her window.

I walked upstairs and went to a window. The rebels were settling themselves as before on the bridge, and sending a boat to the prison ship, when, conceive my astonishment, I saw them all begin to run. I flew downstairs, doubting my senses, to tell Dr Jacob. He came to the window. It was no illusion. Run they did in such confusion that I am amazed numbers were not trampled to death. A general cry, 'The army are come, they are in the town!' explained their flight. Wretches out of the infirmary in their shirts ran in an incredible short space of time. The streets were almost clear . . . The boat that was sent to bring the prisoners to torture and death brought them to liberty and rapture. . . . No kind of *decorum* was observed, nothing but *kissing* and embracing. Most of the men cried violently. I wish that dear General Moore could have seen us. He in reality was two miles off and there were only twelve horsemen in the town, but no one knew that till next day.[10]

Moore described in his diary his arrival in the relieved town:
Upon our approach to the town we saw crowds of people running in all directions out of it. A house on fire made me suspect the rebels meant to burn the town, and perhaps the prisoners in their possession. I therefore advanced and took post close to it, and sent Lord Dalhousie with two hundred men into it, with orders to release the prisoners and leave such a force in the town as would ensure tranquillity and protect the well-affected. The moment I had settled the different regiments I went in myself, and witnessed the most affecting scenes: fathers meeting their children, wives, etc., whom they thought to have perished. Many of the gentlemen, whose families were prisoners in the town, had attended me as guides and yeomen. Forty prisoners had been shot and piked the day before, and it was intended to have shot the rest that evening if I had not come on. They amounted to some hundred persons, of the best rank in the county. I, therefore, had the good fortune to perform one of the most pleasing services that could fall to the lot of an officer.[33]

General Lake's victors at Enniscorthy and Vinegar Hill marched into Wexford the following morning. Lake ordered that the rebel leaders captured should be hanged on Wexford Bridge. Bagenal Harvey escaped capture for a short time by hiding in a cave on an island off the coast.

Sir John Barrington visited Wexford, and, in very different circumstances, gazed on the faces of the radicals who had entertained him on his visit in April.

General Lake . . . had ordered the heads of Mr Grogan, Captain Keogh, Mr Bagenal Harvey, and Mr Colclough, to be placed on very low spikes, over the court-house of Wexford. A faithful servant of Mr Grogan had taken away his head; but the other three remained there when I visited the town. The mutilated countenances of friends and relatives, in such a situation would, it may be imagined, give any man most horrifying sensations! The heads of Mr Colclough and Harvey appeared black lumps, the features being utterly undistinguishable; that of Keogh was uppermost, but the air had made no impression on it whatever! His comely and respect-inspired face (except the *pale* hue, scarcely to be *livid*) was the same as in life: his eyes were not closed – his hair not much ruffled: in fact, it appeared to me rather as a head of chiselled marble, with glass eyes, than as the lifeless remains of a human creature:– this circumstance I never could get any medical man to give me the least explanation of. I prevailed on General Hunter, who then commanded in Wexford, to suffer the three heads to be taken down and buried.[7]

Outside of the province of Leinster, the only serious area of revolt was in the Ulster counties of Antrim and Down, birthplace of the Society of United Irishmen. Yet the challenge there was delayed until the rebels in Wexford were on the way to defeat; nor did the force of the revolt in Ulster match that which brought initial successes to the men of Wexford. When early news of the rebellion reached Tone in France, he was dismayed and perplexed to find no mention of Ulster:

In all this business I do not see one syllable about the North, which astonishes me more than I can express. Are they afraid? Have they changed their opinions? What can be the cause of their passive submission, at this moment, so little suited to their former zeal and energy?[51]

Several reasons could have been given to Tone. The revolutionary spirit had been waning in the North for some time. The savage suppression of 1797 had taken its toll. The rebellion as a whole lacked overall planning, and following the arrests of the Leinster Directory in Dublin co-ordination between South and North broke down. Further, the organization in the North was in disarray. Antrim and Down rose separately, with no linked plan, the latter after the revolt in Antrim was already crushed. Officers in the movement defected, or were halfhearted. The Commanders in each county stepped into their roles at the last minute. The old sectarian divisions were too deep-rooted to be transcended, and there is evidence that the government played on them. The rising in the North was predominantly Presbyterian, with support from the Catholic Defender society. The latter had clashed so often in the countryside with rival Protestant secret societies, such as the Peep-o'-day Boys and the Orangemen, that any alliance between Catholics and Protestants was bound to be a wary one. Catholics drifted away in thousands before the battles in Antrim and Down; and Protestants also defected in large numbers as the sectarian bias of the revolt in County Wexford became known in the North. The government made sure that the massacre of Protestants at Scullabogue and the leadership of priests received maximum publicity in and around Belfast.

A memoir by James Hope, one of the northern United Irishmen, tells how by May 1798 officers in the movement were unreliable.

The organization of the north being thus deranged, the colonels flinched, and the chief of the Antrim men [*Robert Simms*] not appearing, the duty fell on Henry J. McCracken; he sent fighting orders to the colonels of Antrim, three of whom sent the identical orders to General Nugent [*British commander in the North*], and the messenger he sent to Down proving unfaithful, the people of Down had no correct knowledge of affairs at Antrim, until they heard of the battle of 7 June.

The greatest part of our officers, especially of those who were called colonels, either gave secret information to the enemy, or neutralized the exertions of individuals as far as their influence extended. . . .

We were thus situated, forced by burning of houses, and the torturing of the peasantry, into resistance. Without the due appointment of superior officers in the place of those who had resigned and abandoned the cause.[28]

Henry Joy McCracken, a Presbyterian cotton manufacturer, embodied the highest ideals of the Society of United Irishmen, which he had helped to found. He had a pure and passionate belief in political and religious liberty. In Belfast he had opened the first Sunday School open to children of any religious persuasion. But, as we saw in Bagenal Harvey, radical idealism does not equip a man to command armies and fight battles. McCracken's army in County Antrim took Randalstown and Ballymena, smoking the yeomen from their garrison in both places and taking them prisoner. But in the main battle at Antrim, when McCracken led 6,000 men against the garrison of seventy light dragoons, fifty yeomen infantry led by Lord Masserene, and some civilian volunteers, the garrison was able to hold out until in thirty minutes reinforcements arrived from Belfast, and the peasant army was routed. At Randalstown and Ballymena the insurgents had treated the surrendered yeomen humanely; the Crown troops showed no mercy. Upwards of 300 rebels were killed to a government loss of about sixty killed or wounded. Lord O'Neill, governor of the county, was killed: ironically, like Lord Mountjoy killed at New Ross, he had been active for Catholic emancipation.

A grim story is told of the disposal of the rebel dead in sandpits near Lough Neagh. As a cartload of bodies arrived at the pits, a yeoman officer exclaimed: 'Where the devil did these rascals come from?' A reply came in a weak voice from the cart: 'I come frae Ballyboley.' He was buried with the others.

The rebels in Down took to arms two days later, no better equipped for success than their comrades in Antrim. With good judgment, General Nugent, British commander in the North, had not applied the iron hand, and thousands of the United Irishmen stayed in their homes, which were not being burned like those of Catholics in Wexford, given no choice but to take to the fields, hills, and mountains as rebels. In Antrim an immediate amnesty for the handing over of arms and the release of prisoners had ended swiftly the rising in that county. Belfast stayed peaceful. The general for Down, the Rev. Steele Dickson, had been arrested; his replacement, Harry Munroe, an Episcopalian draper from Lisburn, had held no previous rank. A rebel army of about 7,000 men was raised, but gloom about the wisdom of revolt seems to have been widespread among the rank and file. Their spirits rose a little on occupying Newtownards, Saintfield, and other Down towns, and they felt strength of massed numbers when called together to camp on a hill called Ednavady, at Montalto, Lord Moira's demesne, outside Ballynahinch.

The sense of foreboding experienced by those leaving their homes to join the rebellion is imparted in this account by a young man who joined the Newtownards division.

My feelings, on leaving all I held dear, and going to war, from which it was probable I would never return, can be more easily conceived than described. When we mustered at the appointed place to march off, such tender scenes of parting took place that I could have 'played the woman with mine eyes'. We proceeded to Ballyboley, where we were joined by other parties; there I was left by my leader to bring him intelligence, which I was to receive from a messenger who was expected shortly to arrive. I was detained till near sunrise, surrounded by weeping females who had parted with their lovers, brothers, or husbands, expecting never more to behold them. My post therefore was not an agreeable one. I had also the mortification of seeing numbers of the most active propagators of the Union stealing homeward, and leaving the poor fellows whom they had seduced exposed to all the danger.

My elder brother was gone with the body . . . The messenger at length arrived, when we reluctantly parted, and made all the haste possible to overtake the body, by taking through the country to Newtownards, but when I came to Movilla they were flying in all directions. I hastened to join a small party who were collected on the hill, and found my elder brother among them. I learned that, having marched into the town, a volley of fire from the market-house having killed six men, they had all fled. After some deliberation, this small party marched to Conlig, a small hill near Bangor, and there passed the greater part of Sunday, the 10th of June. [*In fact, what had happened was that two groups of rebels in the darkness had each mistaken the other for the enemy. The garrison had already evacuated the town.*]

While here we were reinforced by a considerable number of our friends, and were provided with six swivel three-pounders. In the afternoon we marched into Newtownards, which the military had evacuated, from thence we proceeded to Scrabo, and next morning reached Saintfield. We passed the field where a battle had been fought the previous day. The country people who had fallen were all buried, and they were interring the dead soldiers as we passed. To see a number of my fellow men thrown on a car like dead dogs and cast carelessly into a large pit, filled my mind with gloomy reflections. I had before this only thought of the glories of war, but its horrors had never been taken into consideration.

Monday, and a part of Tuesday, were spent in and about Saintfield; but hearing of the approach of a large party of military, we got the route to Ballynahinch.[2]

The Rev. Dr. Samuel Edgar, Presbyterian minister near Ballynahinch in 1798:

The country was all in motion. Some hesitated what side to join. Some determined to join neither, but were much perplexed in devising means of safety from the soldiers and the people. Goods and furniture were carried to places of concealment. Some left the neighbourhood, and, the better to cover their departure from a scene of disturbance, and to escape in safety, summoned the people, as they themselves retreated from the theatre of action, to turn out and repair to the camp.... At the houses which I passed, some were busy sharpening their pikes and preparing for battle; others, armed with these frightful weapons, were meeting me and crossing my path on their way to the camp.[19]

A fascinated visitor to the rebels' camp was a twelve-year-old boy, James Thomson, son of one of Lord Moira's gardeners. He became Professor of Mathematics in Glasgow University, and father of the future Lord Kelvin.

Immediately on their arrival the insurgents dispatched parties in all directions, for the double purpose of collecting provisions and bringing in the United Irishmen of that part of the country to increase their number. In respect of the latter object they were very unsuccessful; as the men of Ballynahinch and the surrounding country in general chose rather to retire to Slieve Croob [*Mountain*]...

In foraging however the detachments were much more successful: the heaviest threats being denounced against those who would not send prepared provisions to the camp without delay. Hence this part of the mission was in general strictly complied with, chiefly from fear, and perhaps partly from love... A message of the nature above mentioned was delivered to my father's family, as well as to others; and gave immediate employment to the females of the family and such others as could be procured to assist, in preparing oaten cakes and boiling large portions of salted beef and bacon.[50]

Young James accompanied three women carrying provisions to the insurgents' camp.

After a walk of about a mile and a half, a considerable part of which lay in the grounds of Lord Moira, we entered the camp of that body of men who were to sever Ireland from the domination of Britain, and to give her separate existence and a name among the nations – who were to give liberty and equality to their countrymen, to abolish tithes and taxes – in a word to make Ireland at least as happy as the United States and the French Republic were considered, in the ardent conceptions of the republicans of the day.

When we arrived, there were on the ground a considerable number of females, chiefly servants, or the daughters or wives of cottiers or small farmers. These were almost all employed in the same business as themselves; though it is said, that two or three of them remained on the field during the battle . . . two or three young men offered their services to conduct us through the field.

Everything was explained with minuteness: pikes of different constructions were pointed out and their uses explained; cannon and ammunition were shown; the tremendous effects against that, which they were calculated to produce. The leaders were also pointed out . . . The eye was presented with a mixed and motley multitude: some walking about; others stretched listlessly on the green turf along the field; a considerable number sheltering themselves from the scorching rays of a burning sun under the shade of the trees with which the field was skirted. . . . They wore no uniforms; yet they presented a tolerably decent appearance, being dressed, no doubt, in their 'Sunday clothes'. . . . The only thing in which they all concurred was the wearing of green: almost every individual having a knot of ribbons of that colour, sometimes mixed with yellow in his hat. Most of them besides had their hat and button-holes decorated with laurel from the adjoining grounds. Their leaders also in general wore green or yellow belts and some of them green coats. . . . The most common of the decorations were the harp entwined with shamrock or bays, but without the crown. . . .

In their arms there was great diversity as in their dress. By far the majority had pikes, which were truly formidable instruments in close fight. . . . These had generally wooden shafts seven or eight feet long with sharpened heads of steel of different forms and commonly ten or twelve inches in length. . . . Others wore old swords generally of the least efficient kind; and some had merely pitchforks. Those of the higher class were armed with guns. There were also seven or eight pieces of small cannon mounted on common cars which were not calculated to produce much effect.

The army was composed chiefly of persons in youth and middle life . . . All seemed to carry a cheerful expression of countenance . . . The leaders were everywhere moving through the field speaking familiarly and kindly to the men; cheering their courage, and by such stories and jokes as they knew to be suited to their taste, exciting mirth among the groups . . .

We had finished our survey of the camp and were preparing to leave it when on a sudden an alarm was given; and all eyes being instantly directed beyond the town to the road leading from Downpatrick, a detachment of soldiers were distinctly seen approaching at a distance of about three miles. In a moment all was bustle through the fields; and a degree of trepidation and alarm pervaded the undisciplined mass. It is scarcely necessary to state that we instantly quitted the ground. . . .

On arriving home I found the family already in a state of alarm on the top of a high adjoining hill; from the summit of which the movements of both parties were seen with as much accuracy as a distance of about a mile and a half would permit; and the use of a small glass. . . .

According to a preconcerted arrangement two bodies of the King's forces – one from Downpatrick and the other from Belfast – were to meet at a short distance from Ballynahinch, where the two lines of the roads united at the side of a hill opposite to the rebel camp; and the joint force was commanded by General Nugent. If the insurgents had been aware of this arrangement they might easily have defeated the detachment from Downpatrick which arrived more than two hours before the other. Had this been done, it is likely that the detachment from Belfast would either not have ventured to attack them, or failed in gaining a victory; and the fate of the northern insurrection might have been somewhat longer suspended.

As we continued our look-out from the hill the approach of the party from Belfast was in a short time announced by the smoke and flames of the farmhouses which they set on fire indiscriminately on their march from Saintfield to Ballynahinch. . . . On perceiving these acts of devastation all the inhabitants who had not yet deserted their dwellings expected their houses and properties to share the same fate and began forthwith to remove such articles as appeared most valuable, or could be most easily concealed. . . . A person in the neighbourhood concealed upwards of a hundred guineas in a magpie's nest in a high tree. . . .

The two bodies of the military effected a junction without opposition and took their station on an eminence called the Windmill Hill almost exactly on the opposite side of the town and at a distance of nearly a mile from the rebel camp. The battle commenced about six o'clock in the evening and was carried on chiefly by the cannon and musketry till about nine when the conflict ceased in consequence of the darkness. . . . The chief injury sustained by the rebels, however, consisted in a gradual desertion . . . Between two and three o'clock of the morning of Wednesday the horrors of the scene were renewed by the King's forces setting fire to the town, and in a short time a great proportion of the best houses in it were enveloped in flames. . . . This act, which was by no means necessary, caused the rebels immediately to recommence the fight and to endeavour by means of their small artillery to arrest the work of devastation. . . . Some time in the course of the morning the most murderous part of the conflict took place in the streets of Ballynahinch. It is understood that General Nugent sent a strong body with part of the artillery through the town and if possible to drive the rebels from their position by force. To oppose these a party of pikemen were dispatched who were said to have acted with great gallantry and at one time to have possessed themselves of one of the largest of the cannons, which however was shortly afterwards retaken. During this part of the engagement, which continued for a considerable period, we distinctly heard the cheers, the yells and the shrieks of the combatants. . . .[50]

The young man who had earlier left his home to join the rebels with such a sense of foreboding was with the party who entered the town and fought 'with great gallantry' in the streets. Contrary to his expectations, his story ended happily.

When we mustered on a hill south-west of the town our number was so much augmented that I thought it impossible that we could be conquered. But, alas! on the approach of the enemy, all these thoughts vanished. The firing of their cannon no sooner commenced than our men fled in thousands, and when night came on we had not more than a third of our force remaining. Few men were killed on Tuesday evening; but few minds were unclouded by fear. We were reduced to a handful, ill appointed, and undisciplined, exposed to the attack of a regular body of military, well armed, and led by experienced officers. During the night I met my brother, who addressed me nearly in these words:– 'You see we are deserted by all our friends. We must all die early in the morning. If I be killed first, search my pockets and take what money you find, and endeavour to save your own life by flight. If you reach home alive tell my wife how I fell.' He was about a month married, and his words sank deep into my heart. In the morning a tremendous cannonade commenced, which was supported by both sides with great spirit.

We received orders from Munroe, our general, to go foremost into the town, but we refused. Three parties were then sent before us, but before reaching the town they all found means to flinch, and we were obliged to go up in the face of a party of the Monaghan Militia, who did not fail to salute us with a brisk fire. We ran up like bloodhounds, and the Monaghans fled into the town, where they kept up a kind of broken fire, which we returned, although only about twenty of us were armed with muskets. We obliged them to take shelter in the houses twice, but when we attempted to pursue our victory, a cannon which raked the street with grapeshot compelled us to retire.

Our ammunition being spent, and the army receiving fresh supplies, we at last gave way, the 22nd Light Dragoons pursuing us, and killing all they could overtake. In the general confusion I lost my brother, and was shortly after informed that he was fallen. This gave me a new pang of sorrow. However I endeavoured to make the best of my way home, which, after some hardships, I effected. The burning and hanging which followed drove me almost to distraction. One of my dearest comrades lost his life, as well as a great many of my acquaintances.

When I reached home I found my brother there before me. We both escaped punishment, as neither of us had been active in compelling others to rise in rebellion. I now gave up the idea of making amendments in the constitution, and Pope's two lines became my political creed:-

> For forms of government let fools contest,
> Whate'er is best administered is best.[2]

If in several ways the rebellion in the North was a disappointment to Wolfe Tone, there could yet be no gainsaying that, in its freedom from sectarian bias and atrocities of the kind seen in Wexford, it lived up to Tone's ideal of 'the common name of Irishmen', one people regardless of differences of religion. It was this spirit that reappeared during Easter Week, 1916; ironically, when sectarian violence and murder returned to Ireland in the twentieth century, it was in the North.

The French provided a prologue to the 1798 rebellion; they also provided an epilogue. On 23 August, two months too late to help establish the Irish Republic, 1,099 French officers and men, commanded by General Joseph Amable Humbert, landed at Killala, on the wild coast of Mayo. Copies of a proclamation were distributed among the Irish peasants. For those able to read English, it began:

> 'Liberty, Equality, Fraternity, Union
> **IRISHMEN**

'You have not forgot Bantry Bay. You know what efforts France has made to assist you.

'Her affection for you, her desire of avenging your wrongs and assuring your independence can never be impaired.

'After several unsuccessful attempts, behold at last Frenchmen arrived amongst you.

'They come to support your courage, to share your dangers, to join their arms and to mix their blood with yours in the sacred cause of liberty.

'They are the forerunners of other Frenchmen, whom you shall soon enfold in your arms.'[29]

A larger expedition of three thousand soldiers, commanded by General

Hardy, due to sail from Brest, was delayed. Wolfe Tone was with them. Humbert's proclamation ended:

'Union, Liberty, the Irish Republic. Such is our shout. Let us march. Our hearts are devoted to you: our glory is in your happiness.'[29]

The French officers were dismayed by the crudeness of the Irish who joined their army of liberation: in accidentally discharging a musket, one Mayo man nearly shot General Humbert in the head. And the Frenchmen were perplexed to find their political ideas so little understood: it was embarrassing for them to be welcomed as religious crusaders. A French officer told Joseph Stock, Protestant Bishop of Killala:

If they knew how little we care for the Pope or his religion, they would not be so hot in expecting help from us. We have just sent away Mr Pope from Italy, and who knows but we may find him in this country.[45]

The French army, with some Irish support, moved inland and approached Castlebar, the county town, where they expected to meet with formidable opposition. General Lake had just arrived to take command. To the disbelieving despair of their officers – Lord Ormonde burst into tears – the garrison's militia fled before the foreign enemy, some as far as Tuam, forty miles distant, others even farther, to Athlone, sixty-three miles away.

British prestige had to be recovered. William Pitt at once ordered reinforcements to Ireland. In June Lord Camden had been replaced as Viceroy by Lord Cornwallis, who was also appointed Commander-in-Chief. Cornwallis, in trusting the Irish militia, built up by 4 September a force of ten thousand men, mainly regulars. Humbert set up a Provisional Government, and called that every Irishman between the ages of sixteen and forty should rally to the French camp and be prepared to march 'against the common enemy, the Tyrant of Ireland – the English'. Humbert had been assured that the people of the whole country, of every class and faith, would rise and support the French. Nothing of the sort happened: for one thing, the country people were too busy gathering the rich harvest the fine summer had ripened. Hearing of rebel activity in Leitrim, Longford, and Westmeath, but not knowing that the midlands' insurgents had been quickly defeated and scattered,

Humbert took his army across Ireland, telling his men they would be in Dublin in two days. The result was anti-climax: Humbert's army was surrounded by Cornwallis's troops near the village of Ballinamuck, Co. Longford. Humbert fought for half an hour before surrendering his 884 officers and men. In high spirits and singing the 'Marseillaise', the French prisoners were taken on barges in a colourful procession from Tullamore to Dublin, thousands of curious spectators lining the canal banks. In the capital, Humbert and his officers were put up at the best hotel, given a banquet in their honour, then all the French prisoners were sent back to their own country. A fortnight later, a short engagement at Killala, where the rebels held out for an hour, provided the final battle of the rebellion.

Four days before the surrender at Ballinamuck, a small expedition had sailed from Dunkirk, with James Napper Tandy, an Irish rival of Tone, on board. On 16 September Tandy landed at Rutland, Co. Donegal, where the postmaster told him of Humbert's defeat. Tandy distributed a few high-flown proclamations, got drunk with the postmaster, and sailed away with the invasionary force of 270 Grenadiers the next morning.

At sea was the largest of the French expeditionary forces, 2,800 men, General Hardy commanding, from Brest. Wolfe Tone was aboard the flagship, The Hoche, named after the general commanding the frustrated expedition of 1796. On 12 October they were intercepted off the northern coast of Donegal by a British squadron under Sir John Warren. Six of the nine French ships were taken, including the flagship.

Tone faced trial in Dublin on 10 November. He asked one favour of the court – that he should have a soldier's death before a firing-squad. When this request was not granted, he slashed his throat with a razor in his cell, severing his windpipe, not the jugular he intended. To a doctor he whispered: 'I find I am but a bad anatomist.' He died a week later, aged thirty-five.

Three Minor Risings
1803–1848–1867

Oh! breathe not his name, let it sleep in the shade,
Where cold and unhonoured his relics are laid;
Sad, silent and dark be the tears that we shed,
As the night dew that falls on the grass o'er his head.

But the night dew that falls, though in silence it weeps,
Shall brighten with verdure the grave where he sleeps,
And the tear that we shed, though in secret it rolls,
Shall long keep his memory green in our souls.

> Tom Moore, on Robert Emmet, in *Irish Melodies*.

The soldier is proof against an argument but he is not proof against a bullet. The man that will listen to reason, let him be reasoned with, but it is the weaponed arm of the patriot that can alone avail against battalioned despotism (loud cheers).

> Speech by Thomas Francis Meagher, 28 July 1846.
> Reported in the *Nation*, 1 August 1846.

I, A.B., do solemnly swear, in the presence of Almighty
God that I will do my utmost, at every risk, while life lasts,
to make Ireland an independent, democratic republic, that
I will yield implicit obedience, in all things not contrary to the
law of God, to the commands of my superior officers, and that
I shall preserve inviolable secrecy regarding all the transactions
of this secret society that may be confided to me.
So help me God! Amen.

> Fenian Oath, *circa* 1858.

A consequence of the 1798 rebellion was that William Pitt countered the threat of Irish independence by bringing Ireland into the Union. The Irish Parliament voted its own demise, and on 1 January 1801 the United Kingdom of Great Britain and Ireland was born, to last for 120 years. Cornwallis pressed for Catholic Emancipation to be included in the terms of the Union, writing to Pitt:

I certainly wish that England would now make a union with the Irish nation instead of making it with a party in Ireland, and although I agree with those who assert that the Catholics will be immediately converted into good subjects, yet I am sanguine enough to hope, after the most plausible and most popular of their grievances is removed (and especially if it could be accompanied by some regulation of tythes) that we should get time to breathe, and at least check the rapid progress of discontent and disaffection.[14]

But the 'party' (i.e. the Protestant ruling class), still reeling from the shock of the rebellion, had their way and blocked Emancipation. Pitt thought he could bring it in later; but twenty-nine years passed before Catholics could sit in Parliament.

The constitutional and the revolutionary traditions in Irish politics ran together through the nineteenth century. The constitutional campaign for repeal of the Union and for land reforms most held the stage – but the revolutionary current was also there and produced three minor risings: that led by young Robert Emmet in 1803, the Young Irelanders' rebellion of 1848, and the Fenian insurrection of 1867. None of the three provided a serious challenge to the government of its day: none rose much above a brawl with the constabulary: but each made a contribution to the revolutionary tradition and influenced the insurgent patriots of 1916.

In 1803 there was a brief, localized, and seemingly insignificant echo of 1798, when twenty-five-years-old Robert Emmet, a doctor's son and like Tone a Protestant, led a small group of insurgents in an attempt to seize Dublin Castle. Lord Kilwarden, the Lord Chief Justice, and his son-in-law, were piked to death in a coach. Emmet was hanged in the street where the killings occurred. As a patriot who attempted the impossible and gave his life for Irish independence, Emmet was thereafter to sit high in republican affections: not least for an eloquent and impassioned speech from the dock.

My lords, as to why judgment of death and execution should not be passed upon me according to law I have nothing to say; but as to why my character should not be relieved from the imputations and calumnies thrown out against it I have much to say. I do not imagine that your lordships will give credit to what I am going to utter; I have no hopes that I can anchor my character in the breast of the court. I only wish your lordships may suffer it to float down your memories, till it has found some more hospitable harbour to shelter it from the storms with which it is at present buffeted. Was I to suffer only in death after being adjudged guilty, I should bow in silence to the fate which awaits me; but the sentence of the law which delivers over my body to the executioner consigns my character to obloquy. A man in my situation has not only to encounter the difficulties of fortune, but also the difficulties of prejudice. Whilst the man dies, his memory lives; and that mine may not forfeit all claim to the respect of my countrymen, I seize upon this opportunity to vindicate myself from some of the charges alleged against me.

I am charged with being an emissary of France. It is false – I am no emissary. I did not wish to deliver up my country to a foreign power, and least of all to France. Never did I entertain the remotest idea of establishing French power in Ireland. . . . Were the French to come as invaders or enemies, uninvited by the wishes of the people, I should oppose them to the utmost of my strength. Yes! my countrymen, I should advise you to meet them upon the beach, with a sword in one hand and a torch in the other. I would meet them with all the destructive fury of war. I would animate my countrymen to immolate them in their boats before they had contaminated the soil of my country. If they succeeded in landing, and if forced to retire before superior discipline, I would dispute every inch of ground, burn every blade of grass, and the last intrenchment of liberty should by my grave. What I could not do myself, if I should fall, I should leave as a last charge to my countrymen to accomplish; because I should feel conscious that life, even more than death, would be unprofitable when a foreign nation held my country in subjection.... My object, and that of the rest of the Provisional Government was to effect a total separation between Great Britain and Ireland – to make Ireland totally independent of Great Britain, but not to let her become a dependent of France....

Emmet's concluding words are cherished by Irish nationalists:
My lords, you are impatient for the sacrifice. The blood which you seek is not congealed by the artificial terrors which surround your victim; it circulates warmly and unruffled through its channels, and in a little time it will cry to heaven. Be yet patient! I have but a few words more to say – my ministry is now ended. I am going to my cold and silent grave; my lamp of life is nearly extinguished. I have parted with everything that was dear to me in this life for my country's cause, and abandoned another idol I adored in my heart – the object of my affections. My race is run – the grave opens to receive me, and I sink into its bosom. I am ready to die – I have not been allowed to vindicate my character. I have but one request to ask at my departure from this world – it is *the charity of its silence*. Let no man write my epitaph; for as no man who knows my motives dares now vindicate them, let not prejudice or ignorance asperse them. Let them rest in obscurity and peace: my memory be left in oblivion, and my tomb remain uninscribed, until other times and other men can do justice to my character. When my country takes her place among the nations of the earth, then, and not till then, let my epitaph be written. I have done.[20]

John Fisher supplied R. R. Madden with this short description of Emmet's execution:
I saw poor Emmet executed, and immediately before his execution saw him put his hand in his pocket and pull out some silver and some half-pence, which he handed to the executioner, Galvin. Then I saw him take off his cravat with his own hands, hand it to the executioner, and noticed him in the act of addressing Galvin some two or three words. The execution took place at the corner of the lane at St

Catherine's church in Thomas Street, and he died without a struggle. He was immediately beheaded upon a table lying upon the temporary scaffold. The table was then brought down to the market-house, opposite John Street, and left there against the wall, exposed to public view for about two days. It was a deal table, like a common kitchen table.[23]

Padraic Pearse and the patriot insurgents of Easter Week 1916 considered themselves to be the heirs of Tone and of Emmet. Pearse, speaking in 1915 at Wolfe Tone's grave, said: 'No failure, judged as the world judges these things, was ever more complete, more pathetic than Emmet's. And yet he has left us a prouder memory than the men of Brian [Boru] victorious at Clontarf or of Owen Roe victorious at Benburb. It is the memory of a sacrifice Christ-like in its perfection.'

But in the first half of the nineteenth century the people's great hero was Daniel O'Connell, who hated violence and condemned those who favoured it as 'weak and wicked'. In 1823 he founded the Catholic Association, which organized support for parliamentary candidates favouring Catholic Emancipation. He was himself elected for County Clare in 1828, and was able to take his seat in the following year when the government finally granted Catholic Emancipation. O'Connell campaigned for repeal of the Union, holding enthusiastic monster meetings – three-quarters of a million people at Tara in August 1843. After his death in 1847 O'Connell's mass movement broke up, and constitutional methods lost ground to the Young Irelanders, preaching revolutionary tactics to achieve independence.

In January 1847, at the height of the famine deaths, the Young Irelanders founded a militant organization, the Irish Confederation, opening clubs in parishes and towns.

The people's rising in Paris on 22 February 1848 had an inspirational effect on the Young Irelanders. Celebratory bonfires were lit in counties King's, Meath, and Wexford – one at the site of the old rebel camp on Vinegar Hill. The leaders of the Young Ireland movement, who were now planning a rising, were William Smith O'Brien, M.P., aristocrat landlord claiming descent from Brian Boru; Charles Gavan Duffy, editor of the Nation; Thomas Francis Meagher, son of the Catholic Mayor of Waterford; and John Mitchel, son of a Presbyterian minister. Mitchel, in the United Irishman, gave instructions for street fighting in Dublin; and Meagher, in the Nation, called 'up the barricades and invoke the God of battles'.

The rising, when it came, was a romantic affair, relying on a wave of popular feeling to sweep the English into the sea. Much of its character can be caught from a few lines of the high-flying prose of Meagher (known as 'Meagher of the Sword' because of his fiery oratory):

A torrent of human beings, rushing through lanes and narrow streets; surging and boiling against the white basements that hemmed it in; whirling in dizzy circles, and tossing up its dark waves, with sounds of wrath, vengeance and defiance; clenched hands, darting high above the black and broken surface, and waving to and fro, with the wildest confusion in the air; eyes red with rage and desperation, starting and flashing upwards through the billows of the flood; long tresses of hair – disordered, drenched and tangled – streaming in the roaring wind of voices, and, as in a shipwreck, rising and falling with the foam; wild, half-stifled passionate, frantic prayers of hope; invocations, in sobs, and thrilling wailings and piercing cries, to the God of Heaven, His saints, and the Virgin Mary; challenges to the foe; curses on the red flag; scornful, exulting, delirious defiances of death; all wild as the winter gusts at sea, yet as black and fearful, too; this is what I then beheld – these the sounds I heard – such the dream which passed before me!

It was the Revolution, if we had accepted it.

Why it was not accepted, I fear I cannot with sufficient accuracy explain. For, as I have already said, of that whole scene I remember nothing clearly, save the passion, the confusion, and the tumult.[32]

O'Brien and Meagher had gone on a 'raising the country' tour and the above lines referred to the heady scene at Carrick on Suir near Waterford. Two reasons why the Revolution was not accepted was that most Confederates hadn't even a pike to fight with and that the rebels were expected to feed themselves in areas where the peasantry were starving. At Mullinahone, in Tipperary, seven policemen were forced to abandon their barracks; and there was a further encounter with the constabulary at Ballingarry, where two stone-throwing insurgents were shot. But after a week of 'raising the country' Smith O'Brien's rebel 'army' consisted of forty men carrying a few crude weapons. He lamented: 'It matters little whether the blame of failure lies on me or upon others; but the fact is recorded in our annals – that the people preferred to die of starvation at home, or to flee as voluntary exiles to other lands, rather than to fight for their lives and liberties.' But starving peasants, unarmed and with no promise of sustenance, are not the stuff of dashing insurgents. As a result of the potato crop failing from 1845 to 1850 a million people died, and another million emigrated to America. Help on a governmental scale needed to combat the famine was not forthcoming.

The subsequent fortunes of the revolutionaries of 1848 are interesting. Smith O'Brien and Meagher were transported to Tasmania in July 1849. Smith O'Brien, broken in health, was released in 1854 and died ten years later at Bangor, North Wales. In 1852 Meagher escaped to America, where he served as a general in the Southern Army during the Civil War, and in 1867 he was accidentally drowned in the Missouri River while on his way to take up duties as Governor of Montana. Mitchel escaped from Van Diemen's Land to found a newspaper in New York that supported the slave-owners. Charles Gavan Duffy became a Member of Parliament in 1852, representing New Ross. He emigrated to Australia in 1854, where he had a distinguished political career, and was knighted by Queen Victoria in 1873.

Several secret societies aiming to establish an Irish republic existed in 1849. One group actually planned to kidnap Queen Victoria on her visit to Dublin in the summer of that year. On 16 September James Fintan Lalor led a rising in Waterford, which (although in an attack on a police barracks a constable and an insurgent were killed) receives little mention in the history books. Thereafter the hotbed of Irish republican ideas switches for a time to across the Atlantic, where the Fenian Movement was founded in 1855 in New York. Its revolutionary heart was the Irish Republican Brotherhood, the organization which played the leading part in planning the 1916 Rising.

In March 1867 the Fenians staged an ill-coordinated rising in a few parts of Ireland, mainly attacks on police barracks as in 1848. This excerpt from a letter written by Henry Filgate, a member of the

Brotherhood, gives a rapid but adequate glimpse of the character and nature of the revolt:

On the night of March 5, 1867, the boys fell into line in Palmerstown Park, City of Dublin, like veterans, loaded their pieces deliberately, counted off and broke into column like Regulars. An advance guard was thrown out, a rearguard attached, and, when the country permitted, flankers deployed. We could not at any time have been surprised.

Our first prisoners were taken near Milltown, consisting of Sergeant Sheridan and three patrolmen, city police. From these four revolvers, belts, bayonets and spare ammunition were taken.

At Windy Harbor our column was reinforced by a strong detachment of well-armed men, commanded by Captain John Kirwan. Here Kirwan assumed command over all. In the attack of Dundrum Barrack Kirwan was shot through the shoulder, and had to be taken away. The command again fell to [Patrick] Lennon.

This barrack being so near the city we deemed it not wise to remain. Instead we pushed on to Stepaside. Upon nearing this hamlet our column was halted. Sixteen riflemen were detailed to take the barrack. The men being posted, Lennon approached the door of the building, knocked two or three times with the hilt of his sword. He was asked from within: 'Who is there?' He replied: 'I command you to surrender to the Irish Republic.' After a delay the answer came, 'No.' Immediately we were ordered to commence firing through the windows and door. Constable McIlwaine returned the fire. We discovered that the shots came from the second floor. This enabled some of us to get right up to the building, which we did, and with the aid of sledges taken from the village blacksmith shop soon had the lower barricaded window broken in. We could distinctly hear the piercing cries of women coming from the building. We stopped firing the sledging to see if they wanted to come out.

Between their shrieks we could hear a voice calling: 'Are you men of honour?' Lennon replied: 'Yes; we want this barrack and all the Government property it contains, and will make prisoners of war of the men in it.' 'We surrender' came back to us. The door was opened, and we took possession. In ransacking the desk we came across all sorts of legal forms, some made out and ready for service. These we took to the front of the barrack and burned. A 'Peeler' [*policeman*] remarked to a few of us standing by: 'This is awful work in a proclaimed district.' We told him that it was mild to what he would see before the week was out. Alas! Alas! All we could treat them to was to see us lick their comrades on Glencullen Heights the next day.[22]

Most of the leaders of the revolt were captured and sentenced to long terms of imprisonment. In the autumn of 1867 two attempts were made to free Fenians in English prisons: in Manchester a policeman was killed, and in London twelve people were killed and 120 injured in an attempt to dynamite Clerkenwell Prison.

Fenian leader John Devoy said:

Though the Rising of 1867 was a fiasco, it constituted another link in the series of armed revolts against England's domination of Ireland and kept alive the spirit of resistance to that alien rule. . . . it was the example of '67 . . . which made it possible for Ireland in 1916 to reassert in arms its inalienable right to national freedom.[18]

Easter Week 1916

All changed, changed utterly:
A terrible beauty is born.

    W. B. Yeats, *Easter 1916*.

Soldiers are we, whose lives are pledged to Ireland,
Some have come from a land beyond the wave,
Sworn to be free, no more our ancient sireland
Shall shelter the despot or the slave.

    The Irish national anthem.

For my part, as to anything I have done in this, I am not afraid to face either the judgement of God, or the judgement of posterity.

    Padraic H. Pearse.

They carried the stretcher from the ambulance to the jail yard. They put him in a chair.... He was very brave and cool.... I asked him: 'Will you pray for the men who are about to shoot you?' And he answered: 'I will say a prayer for all brave men who do their duty.'... And then they shot him.

    Execution of James Connolly.

Following the failure of the Fenian revolt of 1867, the constitutional campaign for repeal of the union with Great Britain again had the stage to itself. Our interest in the years from 1867 and leading up to the final rebellion in 1916 centres on the struggle for Home Rule. Associated with it was the growth of Irish nationalism, and equally of feelings of separatism among the Protestants in Ulster. Two politicians of great stature were connected with the fight for Home Rule, one English, one Irish: William Ewart Gladstone, the British Liberal leader, Prime Minister 1868–74, 1880–5, 1886, and 1892–4, determined to find a final solution to the 'Irish Question', and the Irish Nationalist Party's leader, Charles Stewart Parnell, who dominated the Irish political scene in the latter half of the nineteenth century the way Daniel O'Connell had done in the first. Parnell was a Protestant, a landlord, and educated in England, but an Irish nationalist, driving for federal Home Rule for Ireland. Building on the foundation laid by Isaac Butt, Parnell brilliantly organized Irish nationalist opinion into a powerful political force.

It was a period when several centuries-old grievances were ended. The Protestant Church of Ireland was disestablished in 1871. But the most important changes were connected with rents and land tenure. Parnell worked with Michael Davitt and the Land League to break the power of the landlords. In September 1880 he called for a 'species of moral Coventry' to be used against persons responsible for eviction. The first victim was Captain Boycott, agent for an absentee landlord – giving a new word to the English dictionary. The land campaign succeeded in pressing from the Government a series of Land Acts which gave security of tenure to tenants who paid rents fixed by courts instead of landlords.

The remaining great national grievance was that Ireland had not her own parliament. Gladstone – one of the few British Prime Ministers to take a keen interest in Ireland – was prepared to grant Home Rule if he could find the necessary parliamentary majority. An opportunity seemed to come with the election of 1885. Parnell returned to Westminster with a Nationalist block of eighty-six members – exactly the same number as the Liberal's majority over the Conservatives. Parnell thus held the balance of power in Parliament. In 1886 Gladstone introduced the First Home Rule Bill, but he was unable to carry his party with him. Ninety-three Liberals voted with the Conservatives, and the bill was defeated on its second reading by thirty votes. Gladstone resigned.

Then came a catastrophe for the Home Rule movement. In December 1889 Parnell was cited in a divorce action brought by a parliamentary colleague, Captain William O'Shea. The court proceedings revealed that Parnell had been living for some years with O'Shea's wife, Kitty, who had borne him children. In the commotion which followed, Gladstone warned the Irish Party at Westminster that they must choose between Parnell or Home Rule, and at a bitter meeting the majority voted for his dismissal as leader. Parnell refused to accept defeat, and the Nationalist Party was split into Pro-Parnell and anti-Parnell factions. Then Parnell died, on 10 October 1891, aged forty-five. His fall was one of the great Irish tragedies.

Gladstone continued to work for Home Rule and forced his second bill through the Commons in 1892, only to have it squashed by the Lords. It was not until 1910, with the Irish members again holding the balance of power in the Commons, that Home Rule once more became a possibility. Gladstone had died in 1898, but the Liberal Party still supported his policy for Ireland. In 1912 Asquith introduced the Third Home Rule Bill. Again it was blocked by the Lords; but Asquith having limited the Lords' power, it was thought likely the Bill could become law by the summer of 1914.

During the period we have covered there was a considerable growth of Irish nationalism and the emergence of a national consciousness that found momentum and expression in such disparate organizations as the Gaelic Athletic Association (1884), the Gaelic League (1893), for studying, preserving, and extending the use of the Irish language, the National Literary Society (1892), and the Abbey Theatre (1897).

When a rising is led by so many poets and intellectuals, Yeats's concern after Easter 1916 –
> Did that play of mine send out
> Certain men the English shot?

– cannot be put down to poetic conceit or hyperbole.

The struggle for Home Rule advanced the growth of national consciousness in the Catholic majority in Ireland; at the same time, opposition to Home Rule developed a sense of separate identity among the Protestants of Ulster: this clash of interests brought the country to the brink of civil war.

In 1886, the year Gladstone introduced the first Home Rule Bill, there was rioting in Belfast. Lord Randolph Churchill gave Ulster's loyalists a slogan: 'Ulster will fight, and Ulster will be right.' Another slogan carrying emotive force was: 'Home Rule means Rome Rule.' In 1893, year of the second Home Rule Bill, a huge Unionist convention was held in Belfast, at which the Duke of Abercorn declared that as a last resort loyalists must be prepared to defend themselves. But the real crisis came in 1912, when Asquith introduced the third Bill, which even if delayed by the Lords was likely to become law by the summer of 1914. In the spring of 1912 more than 100,000 loyalists paraded in Belfast, and there were outbreaks of sectarian violence in the city that summer. The northern unionists had found a determined leader in Sir Edward Carson, a Dublin lawyer. Carson declared that 28 September would be Ulster Day, when loyalists would have the opportunity to dedicate themselves to a solemn covenant, promising to use all the means in their power to resist Home Rule. 471,000 persons signed the covenant that day, some charging the pen with their own blood.

COVENANT

Being convinced in our consciences that Home Rule would be disastrous to the material well-being of Ulster as well as of the whole of Ireland, subversive of our civil and religious freedom, destructive of our citizenship, and perilous to the unity of the empire, we, whose names are underwritten, men of Ulster, loyal subjects of His Gracious Majesty King George V, humbly relying on the God whom our fathers in days of stress and trial confidently trusted, do hereby pledge ourselves in solemn covenant throughout this our time of threatened calamity to stand by one another in defending for ourselves and our children our cherished position of equal citizenship in the United Kingdom, and in using all means which may be found necessary to defeat the present conspiracy to set up a Home Rule parliament in Ireland. And in the event of such a parliament being forced upon us we further solemnly and mutually pledge ourselves to refuse to recognize its authority. In sure confidence that God will defend the right we hereto subscribe our names. And further, we individually declare that we have not already signed this covenant. God save the king.

Preparations were made for a Provisional Government for Ulster, with Carson at its head. Before the signing of the covenant men had been drilling, and in January 1913 the Ulster Volunteer Force was formed, trained by British Army officers, and having its own cavalry, transport, despatch-riders, signallers, and nurses. In March 1914 the majority of British Army officers in Ireland declared that they would resign rather than move their men against the northern loyalists (the Curragh mutiny). On the night of 24 April 1914, 25,000 German rifles and two million rounds of ammunition were landed at Larne, Co. Antrim, and distributed to Volunteers all over Ulster. Augustine Birrell, Chief Secretary for Ireland at the time, recalled:

The famous 'gun-running' exploit in the spring of 1914, though an overt act of rebellion, did not excite in Southern Ireland the same laudable feelings of indignation that it did in constitutional bosoms in England. So far as I could observe, the 'victory' at Larne gave universal satisfaction in Ireland. Was it not an affront to England? Was it not boldly conceived and well executed? Was it not an excellent example? The 'National' Volunteers had no better recruiting-sergeant.

The Irish National Volunteers had been formed by the pro-Home Rulers on 25 November 1913 as a counter to Carson's loyalist force, and included supporters of the Nationalist Party, led by John Redmond, as well as members of more revolutionary bodies, such as Sinn Fein ('ourselves') and the Irish Republican Brotherhood. In emulation of the U.V.F., the National Volunteers landed German arms and ammunition in Ireland, at Howth, near Dublin, on 26 June 1914. On 4 August, with Ireland on the brink of civil war, Great Britain declared war against Germany, who had invaded Belgium.

The Ulster Volunteers were incorporated into the British Army as the 36th (Ulster) Division, and suffered immense casualties in the slaughter of the Somme. An almost equal number of National Volunteers joined the British Army. Redmond called on them to support Britain in 'a just war provoked by the intolerable military despotism of Germany'. Seventeen V.C.s were won by Irishmen in the first year of the war. But Britain's difficulty was once again offering a revolutionary opportunity for some Irishmen.

The republican faction among the National Volunteers objected to Redmond's recruiting for the British Army, and twenty members of the committee broke away to form their own force, known as the Irish or Sinn Fein Volunteers. Leader of the new group was Eoin MacNeill, a civil servant, co-founder of the Gaelic League. Main support was in Dublin, where nearly one-third of the I.N.F. joined the breakaway group. When the most revolutionary among them planned a national rising for 24 April 1916, MacNeill was kept in the dark. And for once spies and informers failed their masters at Dublin Castle.

The Irish Republican Brotherhood sought military support from the Germans for the Irish rising. A former British diplomat, Sir Roger Casement, reached Germany and attempted with little success to raise an Irish Brigade from Irish prisoners of war to join in the insurrection. The Germans agreed to send a ship to Ireland carrying 20,000 rifles, ten machine-guns, and five million rounds of ammunition – but refused to supply men. Casement tried in vain to get word to friends in Ireland that the rising should be postponed, but that the German arms should be landed and distributed. Disguised as a Norwegian trawler, the German ship reached Tralee Bay on the afternoon of Thursday, 19 April, but was not recognized by the pilot of the contact vessel who had been told to expect the German ship on Sunday. It sailed away, but was captured by the Royal Navy. On being taken into the harbour at Queenstown, the German captain ran up his national colours and scuttled the ship. Meanwhile, that same morning, Casement had landed from a submarine on Banna strand in County Kerry. Within a few hours he was picked up by the police: his trousers were coated with wet sand and in his pocket was a used railway ticket from Berlin to Wilhelmshaven.

The Press Bureau released the news late on 24 April:

ARREST OF SIR ROGER CASEMENT

The Secretary of the Admiralty announces:

During the period between p.m. April 20 and p.m. April 21 an attempt to land arms and ammunition in Ireland was made in a vessel under the guise of a neutral merchant ship, but in reality a German auxiliary, in conjunction with a German submarine. The auxiliary sank, and a number of prisoners were made, among whom was Sir Roger Casement.[43]

It was not until Thursday, 20 April that Eoin MacNeill found out about the planned insurrection, and, considering it would, be a hopeless slaughter, set about trying to call it off. He sent messengers to many places in Ireland carrying his order to cancel the manoeuvres organized as a cover for the national rising, and also placed an advertisement to that effect in the Sunday Independent, *the Sunday newspaper with the largest circulation, for 23 April.*

Owing to the very critical position, all orders issued to the Irish Volunteers for tomorrow, Easter Sunday, are hereby rescinded, and no parades, marches, or other movements of Irish Volunteers will take place. Each individual Volunteer will obey this order strictly in every particular.

Eion MacNeill.[43]

The effect of MacNeill's countermanding order to the Volunteers was to cut down the scope of the insurrection, but not to halt it. Its effect on the top Government officials was to make them think the holiday weekend would pass as relaxed and peaceful as the sunny weather seemed to indicate.

MONDAY 24 APRIL

To the citizens of Dublin the events that began at noon on Easter Monday 1916 were startling melodrama.

Mr E. A. Stoker, a jeweller in Grafton Street, was passing the General Post Office in Sackville Street (now O'Connell Street), when he . . .

... noticed a mixed crowd of, I should say, roughly, about one hundred men and boys, all armed, and half the number carrying old portmanteaux and parcels of every description. It is said that Connolly was leading. He called 'Halt! Left turn! Come on.' The crowd then ran into the Post Office. I also followed. Several men crossed the counter and held revolvers at the officials' heads. One youth, intensely pale and nervous, put a revolver at my breast and said, 'Clear out.' I replied, 'What's up?' He said, 'Hands up, or I'll blow your heart out.' Up went my hands, and he backed me out to the entrance, and within five minutes everybody else had been bundled out in the same unceremonious way, and they were in possession.[46]

Playwright St John Ervine was in the Abbey Theatre when he heard that something extraordinary was happening at the G.P.O. He left the theatre and walked the short distance to Sackville Street.

I looked across the street, and saw that the windows of the Post Office had been broken. Furniture and sacking were piled behind every window, and stretched on top of these were boys with rifles, lying there, waiting. Some of the rebels were distributing bills, in which the heads of the Provisional Government announced the establishment of an Irish Republic.[21]

PROCLAMATION OF THE REPUBLIC

Irishmen and Irishwomen: In the name of God and of the dead generations from which she receives her old tradition of nationhood, Ireland, through us, summons her children to her flag and strikes for her freedom.

Having organized and trained her manhood through her secret revolutionary organization, the Irish Republican Brotherhood, and through her open military organizations, the Irish Volunteers, and the Irish Citizen Army, having patiently perfected her discipline, having resolutely waited for the right moment to reveal itself, she now seizes that moment, and, supported by her exiled children in America and by gallant allies in Europe, but relying in the first on her own strength, she strikes in full confidence of victory.

We declare the right of the people of Ireland to the ownership of

Ireland, and to the unfettered control of Irish destinies, to be sovereign and indefeasible. The long usurpation of that right by a foreign people and government has not extinguished the right, nor can it ever be extinguished except by the destruction of the Irish people. In every generation the Irish people have asserted their right to national freedom and sovereignty; six times during the past three hundred years they have asserted it in arms. Standing on that fundamental right and again asserting it in arms in the face of the world, we hereby proclaim the Irish republic as a sovereign independent state, and we pledge our lives and the lives of our comrades-in-arms to the cause of its freedom, of its welfare, and of its exaltation among the nations.

The Irish republic is entitled to, and hereby claims, the allegiance of every Irishman and Irishwoman. The republic guarantees religious and civil liberty, equal rights and equal opportunity to all its citizens, and declares its resolve to pursue the happiness and prosperity of the whole nation and of all its parts, cherishing all the children of the nation equally, and oblivious of the differences carefully fostered by an alien government, which have divided a minority from the majority in the past.

Until our arms have brought the opportune moment for the establishment of a permanent national government, representative of the whole people of Ireland, and elected by the suffrages of all her men and women, the Provisional Government, hereby constituted, will administer the civil and military affairs of the republic in trust for the people. We place the cause of the Irish republic under the protection of the Most High God, whose blessing we invoke upon our arms, and we pray that no one who serves that cause will dishonour it by cowardice, inhumanity, or rapine. In this supreme hour the Irish nation must, by its valour and discipline, and by the readiness of its children to sacrifice themselves for the common good, prove itself worthy of the august destiny to which it is called.

Signed on behalf of the provisional government,

Thomas J. Clarke, Sean MacDiarmada, Thomas MacDonagh, P. H. Pearse, Eamonn Ceannt, James Connolly, Joseph Plunkett.[43]

The two leading figures in the insurrection were contrasts in background amd personality. Padraic H. Pearse, aged thirty-seven, came from an upper middle-class family. His father was English, his mother Irish. For a short time he practised as a barrister, but disliked the profession. He wrote poetry, in Gaelic and in English. At the time of the rising he was headmaster of St Enda's, a bilingual college. Though unsuited to a military role, his spirituality and integrity (today's journalists would call it 'charisma') landed him the position of Commander-in-Chief. In contrast, James Connolly, aged forty-five, came from a working-class background. He was born in County Monaghan, and had the speech and directness of an Ulsterman. He was realistic and practical, and had served in the British Army. He was a vigorous writer and debater on Socialism, and head of the Irish Citizen Army, a workers' defence force set up after clashes between workers and police during the tramwaymen's strike in Dublin in 1913. Another significant signatory to the proclamation, Tom Clarke, kept a tobacconist's shop near the G.P.O. in Dublin; sixteen of his fifty-nine years had been spent in English jails. Another who had known imprisonment was Sean MacDermott (MacDiarmada); he was crippled and walked with the aid of a stick. Thomas MacDonagh, aged thirty-eight, a tutor at University College, Dublin, was a close friend of Pearse, and, like him, a poet. Another poet was Joseph Plunkett, aged twenty-four, son of a papal count, frail and consumptive. Eamonn Ceannt (Edmund Kent), aged thirty-five, was a clerk in the City Treasurer's office. In this mixture of types of men, nothing quite like it can be found in any comparable insurrection in history.

To St John Ervine, looking across the street to the G.P.O. on Easter Monday, the whole business had an unreal, theatrical quality that was somehow juvenile.

Someone began to deliver an oration at the base of the Nelson pillar, but the crowd had no taste for oratory, and it did not listen long. There were two flags on the top of the Post Office, a green one, bearing the words 'Irish Republic', and a tricolour of orange, white, and green; and that was all. One saw Volunteer officers carrying loaded revolvers, passing about their duties, instructing pale boys who were acting as sentinels; and when one saw how young they were, there came into the mind that sense of the ridiculousness of it all, and one thought, 'This is all very well, this playing with rebellion and establishing a republic; but wait – just wait until the police catch you at it!' One thought of them as boys who had let their lark run away with their wits.... 'It'll be over when dinner-time comes,' someone said to me. We were all extraordinarily lacking in prescience. We still thought of this thing as a kids' rebellion, a schoolboys' escapade. 'Silly young asses!' people were saying, 'they'll only get into trouble.'[21]

Louis George Redmond-Howard, on the balcony of the Metropole Hotel, looking across to the Post Office, was struck by the lack of popular support for the republicans. He ...

... was able to secure a unique snapshot of the hoisting of the new flag of the Republic, and took another of the cheering of the crowd – though this was very insignificant and in no way represented any considerable body of citizens, any of the better class having disappeared, leaving the streets to idlers and women and children or else stray sightseers.... I realized at once that the movement was at that time a dismal failure as far as the vast majority of Nationalist Ireland was concerned. There was practically no response whatever from the people: it seemed the very antithesis of the emancipation of a race as we see it, say, in the capture of the Bastille in the French Revolution. They looked on partly with amazement, partly with curiosity – waiting for something dramatic to happen.[40]

This turned out to be the advance of a troop of Lancers to near Nelson's Pillar – the rebels opened fire from the Post Office, bringing down horses, killing four troopers, and scattering the rest. Cavalry were not the right troops to dislodge the barricaded insurgents. Casualties would have been greater if the rebels had not been impatient and opened fire before Connolly gave the command. Connolly had served some years in the British Army, and soon showed himself to be a cool and skilled commander. Riflemen, on his orders, occupied houses around the Post Office. Telegraph wires were cut to make communication difficult for the authorities and the military. The rebels had some one-way wireless equipment.

Apart from firing upon the Lancers, the insurgents in their great

granite headquarters had no other encounters with the enemy on Monday.
Leaving Sackville Street, St John Ervine walked up Grafton Street to St Stephen's Green.

I walked along the Green toward the Shelbourne Hotel. Inside the railings I could see boys digging trenches and throwing up heaps of earth for shelters. Other boys were stretched on the turf, with their fingers on the triggers of their rifles, and they, too, like the boys at the Post Office were waiting. I heard a man say to one lad who was digging into the soft earth: 'What in the name of God are you doin' there?' And the lad replied: 'I don't know. I'm supposed to be diggin' a trench, but I think I'm diggin' my grave.'[21]

Brian O'Higgins was a private with a group of Volunteer reserves who called themselves the 'lame ducks' because their poor state of health or physical handicaps had excused them from 'the heavy work that had to be done by every man in the ranks'. Nevertheless, they turned up at the G.P.O. on Easter Monday.

At half-past ten word came to me that a man who had ridden up hurriedly on a bicycle was waiting to see me at the gate. He was the man who had been told off to mobilize the section of the Reserve Co. to which I belonged. . . . I did not wait to put on my uniform, fearing I would not be in the city in time, and my gun and ammunition being there since the day before, I simply took my rations, got out my bike and started. We met at the appointed place; we heard of the disaster in Kerry and the arrest of 'Ruairi na nGaedheal', the noble-hearted Roger Casement, but we heard also the first volley that was fired from the General Post Office, saw the Lancers galloping home to barracks in great haste, and our hearts were glad. The blow had at last been struck. . . . On our way to the G.P.O. that evening we met at least half-a-dozen soldiers in khaki walking freely through the streets. Some of the lads who were with us were just yearning to fire a shot . . . but the English soldiers were not on active service at the time and they were unarmed, and the Irish Volunteers did not believe in firing on unarmed men. . . . At the G.P.O., when our little band marched in, we were welcomed by Pearse himself, who smilingly told us he had almost forgotten all about us. An air of quiet jubilation pervaded the whole place. Men's eyes shone with a light they had never known before, hands were gripped in welcome in joy and congratulation, and on every lip was heard a prayer of thanks to God that the day had come at last.[39]

Due to his poor state of health, O'Higgins was taken off sentinel duty on the edge of the sidewalk between the great pillars of the Post Office and given indoor work.

Hour by hour and bit by bit news that thrilled our hearts came in from every part of the city. Our men – a mere handful – had routed the enemy at Fairview after a sharp encounter on Annesley Bridge; three hundred British soldiers had been driven back into Portobello Barracks by nine men; MacDonagh had taken possession of Jacob's Biscuit Factory and was putting up a big fight there; the Citizen Army under Mallin occupied the St Stephen's Green area; Sean Connolly had taken the City Hall; Ned Daly held the Four Courts and a big neighbouring area; Eamon de Valera was in possession at Westland Row Railway Station, at Boland's Mill, at Ringsend and at every point commanding the roads from Dunlaoghaire [*then Kingstown*]; Sean Heuston was in the Mendicity Institute on the quays; Cathal Brugha was making a magnificent fight in the South Dublin Union; Eamonn Ceannt held Marrowbone Lane Distillery; Thomas Ashe had mobilized North Dublin County; the boys of Wexford were following in the footsteps of the men of 1798; the men of the West had raised the tricolour in Galway, and Liam Mellows had come back from his enforced exile to lead them ...[39]

The cock-a-hoop spirits of the rank-and-file Volunteers were understandable. Almost unopposed, they had occupied key positions in the city, and little or no attempts had been made to dislodge them.

To Mrs Norway, wife of the Post Office Secretary, staying at the Royal Hibernian Hotel in Russell Street, the unpreparedness of the Government was appalling. When she heard that the G.P.O. had been taken over by insurgents, her anxiety over the safety of her husband was acute. She sent out her son, Nevil, to see if he could contact his father. The mother's diary offers more immediate and vivid pen-pictures than the memoirs of the son, even though the latter became a best-selling novelist (Nevil Shute).

About one-thirty N. returned, having failed to find any trace of

H., but he had seen some cavalry shot coming out of Talbot Street into Sackville Street. The first three or four were just picked off their horses and fell wounded or dead, and the horses were shot. He said the scene of excitement in Sackville Street was indescribable. We were just going to lunch when a telephone message came through saying H. was at the Castle but could not leave.

This relieved our minds as to his fate, and after lunch I was kept busy at the telephone answering distracted messages from Post Office officials who were wandering about looking for H. At about 4 p.m. N. returned from a tour of inspection, and told me all was quiet in Sackville Street, and begged me to go with him to the G.P.O. ... Over the fine building of the G.P.O. floated a great green flag with the words 'Irish Republic' on it in large white letters. Every window on the ground floor was smashed and barricaded with furniture, and a big placard announced the 'Headquarters of the Provisional Government of the Irish Republic'. At every window were two men with rifles, and on the roof the parapet was lined with men. H.'s room appeared not to have been touched, and there were no men at his windows.

We stood opposite and were gazing, when suddenly two shots were fired, and, seeing there was likely to be an ugly rush, I fled again, exhorting N. to take refuge at the club.

He never reached the club, but came back to the hotel, and we had tea, and he then went to inspect St Stephen's Green.

He found all round the Green, just inside the railings among the shrubberies, the rebels had dug deep pits or holes, and in every hole were three men. They had barricaded the street opposite the Shelbourne Hotel, and there had been a lot of firing and several people killed, and shots had gone into the hotel ...

All the evening we heard firing in all directions of the city and rumours of troops having arrived from the Curragh. While at dinner another message came through from H. to say we were not to be alarmed; he was quite safe, but might not get home that night.

After dinner N. went out to see if he could get near the Castle, but he found awful fighting. The troops were storming the City

Hall and using machine-guns, and it was too 'unhealthy' for him to get near, so he came back at nine and went to bed.

I stayed up in case of being wanted on the 'phone, and at 11.30 p.m. went up to my room, and a few minutes later H. walked in, to my immense relief.

The troops had arrived from the Curragh at about five p.m. and had promptly stormed the City Hall, which commanded the main gate of the Castle, and had taken it after fierce fighting. H. saw prisoners being brought into the Castle yard, and when all was quiet he and several other officials crept out and reached their various homes.

People are appalled at the utter unpreparedness of the Government. In the face of a huge body of trained and armed men, openly revolutionary, they had taken no precautions whatever for the defence of the city in the event of an outbreak. At the beginning of the war H. obtained a military guard, armed, for the G.P.O., and they have always been there. When the outbreak occurred yesterday the armed guard were there, but with no ammunition. The sergeant was wounded in two places and the rest overpowered.[35]

MacNeill's cancellation of the Volunteer's manoeuvres, coming on top of the arrest of Casement and the seizure of the German arms ship, all contributed to what in retrospect seems a lack of alertness in the officials of Dublin Castle. Though Birrell had conceded the possibility of 'a real street row and sham rebellion in Dublin', and the Under-Secretary, Sir Matthew Nathan, had warned of growing support for Sinn Fein, the Rising took them, and therefore the military, by surprise. Only Lord Wimborne, the Viceroy, seems to have been alive to the danger, for on Easter Sunday he told Nathan that he wanted 'between sixty and a hundred of the ringleaders arrested tonight'. If this had been done, the Rising is unlikely to have happened, or been reduced to Birrell's 'street row'. Nathan was unwilling to act until he had contacted and consulted with Birrell, who was out of Dublin that weekend. On Easter Monday at the Castle top officials were discussing the question of arrests, and the significance of Casement's landing and capture, when an unarmed policeman at one of the Castle's gates was shot dead and the Rising began. If the rebels had pressed home their attack – instead of taking up sniping positions in the City Hall – the symbol of British rule for centuries should have fallen; for less than a score of men were in the garrison.

A dramatic attempt had been made to blow up the Magazine Fort in Phoenix Park. By accident, the key of the main explosives' store was in the pocket of an officer who had gone to the races at Fairyhouse. The explosion was minor, and the rebels made off with some rifles in (of all things) a jaunting-car. The seventeen-year-old son of the Fort's commander was shot dead as he ran to give the alarm.

The insurgents in Dublin had occupied strong defensive positions, but the British Army Commander's tactics were to throw a cordon around the centre of the city and to rely on artillery, reinforced by a gunboat on the Liffey, to batter the rebels into submission. Time was on the side of the Government.

There had never been a stranger day in Dublin's history.

TUESDAY 25 APRIL

The following impressionistic record of what it was like for one of the rebels occupying the G.P.O. was smuggled out of jail shortly after the surrender.

Marched according to orders to Liberty Hall with small company in which I drilled, little expecting to be so soon in arms against the armed forces of Great Britain. Great excitement prevailed and the surrounding area was desolate in appearance. The door is locked. Congestion of traffic has whetted our curiosity as we marched through the average holiday crowds and soldiers strolling with their girls past College Green. Admitted to Larkin's palace we swarm upstairs. The Volunteers are 'out' and Ireland is rising. It is evident from the excited shouts to keep 'a watch on the railway line' and 'fill all vessels with water'. Rifles and flushed faces. A feeling of momentary sickness, then wonder. An excited youth informs our Commander that there are no longer Volunteers or Citizen Army, so Mr Connolly had said when the row started and the Volunteers had been addressed in front of the Hall, only the Army of the Irish Republic. Commandant Pearse sends down a message to us to proceed to the G.P.O. We hurry downstairs and at the double across Abbey Street. 'Hurrah for the Volunteers!' shouts an aged working man. 'Hammer the s—— out of the ——!' We rush across Princes Street catching a glimpse of a girl crying and hurrying along, a well-dressed young man beside her. People cheer from doorways. A dim crowd up towards the Rotunda. The G.P.O. windows loom before us, men inside with rifles behind barricaded windows. Our Commander's rifle-butt smashes through glass and wood and breaks. Scramble in and over. Shots ring deafeningly in our ears. A cry, 'the Lancers!' and a volley from within to stop those troops who retire, leaving two dead horses behind. Hurry. Locks blown in, men rush to the roof, to the second storey. Sacks, books, typewriters are stuffed in all hitherto not strengthened windows. Men watch grimly behind. Pearse and his brother appear and survey the scene calmly within, though the latter looks a trifle sad. Vessels are filled with water everywhere. Cooking is carried on where the G.P.O. staff left off. The great leading door into Princes Street is eventually covered with a rough barricade. A young officer dashes in cheering, a smile on his flushed features. Later he is hurried by, the lower part of his face severely injured with a bomb explosion, his hands, chin and neck streaming blood. He is ordered at the revolver's point – for he grows obstinate – when his wounds are dressed and the shock subsides – to hospital. Blood is new to us and we only learn later that he is recovered. Inside organization proceeds. Parties come and go. The crowd outside cheers the hoisted Republican flags and the Proclamation. Pearse speaks without. Connolly, a grim, manly figure in green Commandant's uniform grasps his hand: 'Thank God, Pearse, we have lived to see this day!' An orderly desolation has settled down within. A dazed D.M.P. man sits in the yard, florid, his head between his hands, but plucks up courage to ask the rebels for beer as he has five children and one wife. He doesn't get anything but kindness. Ambulances draw up outside and bear away wounded brought in. The Cumann na mBan girls soon, however, have set up a hospital on the ground floor in a former sorting-room. Henry Street corner and block opposite are gradually occupied by Volunteers. Gunshots and startling rumours of Ireland ablaze are as common as rosary beads round the necks of the watchers on the windows. Fires start opposite, are quenched, begin again and we grow used to the flames leaping up as we fall into brief spells of sleep or face the whizzing bullets whistling past and around us. Pop-pop-pop. Machine-guns are destroying Liberty Hall. Boom! Boom! Heavier guns. We get used to them. But before that we have seen looting without, heard heavy firing in the sleepless nights, stood to arms to resist the long expected general assault, seen Volunteers sally out on 'death and glory' missions, or simply with revolvers and batons to suppress the looters whom MacDermott has appealed to on several occasions.[42]

The looting presented some bizarre sights. Louis George Redmond-Howard:

After Noblet's [*toffee shop*], it was the Saxone Shoe Co.'s and Dunn's hatshop's turn to be looted, and one could see little guttersnipes wearing high silk hats and new bowlers and straws, who had never worn headgear before: barefooted little devils with legs buried in Wellington top-boots, unable to bend their knees, and drunken women brandishing satin shoes and Russian boots till it seemed the whole revolution would collapse in ridicule or pandemonium. For there was no animosity in the crowd at first, just as there was no enthusiasm – certainly no avarice or desire for theft – only sheer demoralization and mischief for mischief's sake: but every hour it became worse. Sometimes there was absolutely no point in the loot. I saw an urchin of nine brandishing with pride More's *Utopia* and Well's *New Machiavelli*, which he compared with a rival urchin's – a girl's – bunch of newspapers on *Poultry* and *Wireless*, and solemnly exchanging their treasures. I saw a tussle between two drunken harlots for the possession of a headless dummy taken from a tailor's shop, and noted a youngster go up to the very steps of the Provisional Government House of the New Republic of Ireland and amuse the armed rebels with impersonations of Charlie Chaplin.[40]

The looting was a regrettable sight to the men occupying the Post Office. Brian O'Higgins felt called on to explain – A great deal of looting took place in the vicinity of the G.P.O., but it would have taken more than our entire garrison to prevent it. Our leaders did their best, but it was no easy matter to cope with the like at such a time – *and related a humorous story told by a priest.* Many priests exposed themselves to the fire of the enemy in an effort to stop the looting, and but for them it would very probably have been more extensive. One of them tells a very good story in this connection. He was hurrying down Parnell Square to where the looting was going on when he met a young barefooted boy hurrying home with an armful of high-class boots. The good priest thought he might as well begin his work there and then. 'Where did you get those boots, boy?' he demanded. The boy looked over his shoulder but kept on hurrying. 'In Earl Street Father,' says he, 'but you'll have to hurry up or they'll be all gone!'[39]

In Sackville Street, when the worst of the looting was taking place, St John Ervine came across Francis Sheehy-Skeffington, who, with his red beard and flowing locks, knickerbocker tweed suit, and loose umbrella, was a well-known 'character' of the Dublin scene. He was an ardent champion of the causes of socialism, pacifism, and women's suffrage. His death during Easter Week, at the hands of a mad British officer, provided one of the most shocking events of the rebellion.

Francis Sheehy-Skeffington came up to me. He had half a dozen walking-sticks under his arm, and he said to me: 'I'm trying to form a special constabulary to prevent looting. You'll do for one,' and he offered a walking-stick to me. I looked at the stick and I looked at the looters, and I said, 'No'. It was characteristic of 'Skeffy', as he was called in Dublin, that he should behave like that. The pacifist in him would not permit him to use force to restrain the looters, though one might have thought that the logician in him would have regarded a walking-stick as a weapon; but the hero in him compelled him, for the honour of his country, to do something to restrain them. . . . I imagine that he was unsuccessful in his efforts, for later on in the afternoon I saw him pasting slips of paper on the walls of O'Connell Bridge. The slips bore an appeal to men and women of all parties to attend the offices of the Irish Suffrage Society in Westmoreland Street and enrol themselves as special constables to maintain order. That evening he was taken by a lunatic officer and shot in Portobello Barracks.[21]

The officer concerned, Captain J. C. Bowen-Colthurst, had been showing signs of strained and strange behaviour for some time. On Tuesday evening, before going to sleep at Portobello Barracks, he read the Bible, and a passage from St Luke clinched the fate of Sheehy-

Skeffington and two journalists also held at the barracks. 'But those mine enemies, which would not that I should reign over them, bring hither and slay before me.' Bowen-Colthurst had the three men shot in the morning. He was court-martialled in June, found guilty but insane, and released after a year.

During the early hours of Tuesday further troop reinforcements from the big military camp at the Curragh had arrived in Dublin. With them was Brigadier-General Lowe, given command of the British Forces in the Dublin area.

The rebels had cause to regret not occupying Trinity College. Only eight armed men had been in it on Monday afternoon. The building was strategically situated between the rebel occupations of the G.P.O. and St Stephen's Green. The military occupied the College with infantry, cavalry, and artillery, and from the upper windows were able to direct machine-gun fire on Sackville Street and the G.P.O.

At St Stephen's Green the rebels were exposed to machine-gun fire from the Shelbourne Hotel and other buildings overlooking the Green. After suffering casualties, Commandant Michael Mallin ordered a withdrawal of most of his men to the Royal College of Surgeons. Second in command in this area was the fiery Countess Markievicz.

Meanwhile, at the General Post Office, the insurgents remained comparatively undisturbed. Brian O'Higgins:

Tuesday night came word of an attack on our position in force, and preparations were made to meet it. All lights were extinguished, every point from which a shot could be fired or a hand-grenade thrown was manned; while reserves were held in readiness to take the places of their comrades, if necessary, and the order was 'fight to the death'. If the enemy succeeded in breaking in by any of the doors every inch of the building was to be contested, and not a man was to lay down his arms until he laid them down in death. . . . The attack in force did not come that night or any other night, but if it had been attempted the enemy would have paid a big price for his trouble, and the chances were that after losing hundreds of men he would have been obliged to retire, for the G.P.O. was a fortress that could not easily be taken and the garrison were prepared to sell their lives dearly.[39]

WEDNESDAY 26 APRIL

On Easter Tuesday, Maurice Headlam, the Treasury Remembrancer, phoned the Castle . . .

. . . not expecting to get an answer. But the rebels, though they had occupied the Post Office, had forgotten to do anything about the telephones, and, after some time, I got on to Sir Mathew Nathan, the Under-Secretary. He replied guardedly to my eager questions that the situation was well in hand, and that there was no need for me to go to the Castle. Then he rang off, and we were no wiser. . . . That night the skies were red with the fires in Dublin . . . I determined, whatever happened, that I ought to go into Dublin and see whether my lodgings in Stephen's Green were safe, and also my office and my office-keeper and his family at the Castle.

Accordingly, on the next morning, Wednesday, I borrowed Anthony's bicycle, taking some food with me in case my landlady had not been able to obtain any. One has to cross the Canal and one of several bridges to get into Dublin from Belgard, and as I approached the bridge on the direct road I saw that the sides were lined with soldiers in khaki, taking cover and shooting across the canal. I turned round and tried the next bridge, which was unoccupied by soldiers or rebels, and came in by Earlsfort Terrace. [*He left the bicycle at the house of a friend.*] Earlsfort Terrace runs into Stephen's Green, and, at the entrance to the Green, there was much sound of shooting. I did not want to be shot, but the firing seemed on the Harcourt Street side of the Green and I determined to go on. Not a soul was to be seen in the streets, the blinds of the houses were all down, there was a wrecked tramcar on the rails halfway down the Green, and then I saw soldiers firing from the roof of the Shelbourne Hotel at the end of the Green facing me, and shots were coming at them from the Harcourt Street end. . . . I mustered up enough courage to stroll along leisurely while the battle went on overhead, till, without being shot at by either side, I reached my house, outside which, on the tram-lines, lay a dead horse . . . I . . . noticed many bullet marks on the outside of the house while I knocked. My landlady was much agitated but no damage had been done and they had been able to get food. I told her that I was trying to get to the Castle

... I then slipped into the United Arts Club next door and had some talk with St John Ervine. . . . Meanwhile the firing seemed to have stopped and a few people were creeping about. . . .

A little knot had gathered outside my house, at the edge of the Green railings, and I went across the road. It seemed that there was a dead Sinn Feiner there, and some young men were talking about giving him a decent burial when an old woman screamed – 'Let the carrion rot, bringing disgrace on the fair name of Ireland!' It seemed as if the 'people' were sound.[26]

From the window of the United Arts Club, Headlam saw ...

... a little procession of nurses, and one or two men evidently doctors, walking in the direction of the Castle. This seemed to me a chance. I ran out and asked the man at the head of the party if they were going to the Castle, and when he said yes, I explained that I wanted to go there and asked if I might walk with them. He hesitated, but I took one of the bags he carried, saying that it was most important for me to get to the Castle. I thought that neither side would fire on nurses. At the Lower Castle Yard gate the sentry let us in without difficulty; there was no incident in the deserted streets on the way, and I thanked my conductors and went on my way to the Lower Castle yard. It was bright sunlight and a lot of soldiers were sitting with their rifles, smoking peacefully, against the wall of the houses at right angles to the terrace of my office. Occasional bullets, coming, as I afterwards found, from Jacob's Biscuit Factory, which the Sinn Feiners had taken, whined over their heads, but no one seemed to be replying to the fire.

My office-keeper, a nice man who had been one of Arthur Balfour's footmen when he was Chief Secretary, was rather flurried. He said that his children – he lived below my office – were much frightened: a Sinn Feiner had been killed by the soldiers on the roof of the office and not taken away. Nothing had been damaged in my office, but no one had come to work. No one was allowed into the Castle, so, if they had tried to come, they would have been turned away. He told me that the Under-Secretary was in the stable block, the buildings against which the soldiers were sitting, under cover from the firing from Jacob's. I went to the door and asked for the Under-Secretary, whom I found busily writing, as usual, and quite calm. He gave me no information about the origin of the outbreak, said reinforcements were on the way and it would soon be over, but that there would be no possibility of work for a day or two. . . .

Things were much quieter, and I got to the Club without incident. I noticed that the dead horse was still lying outside my house, and, thinking that it would be a nuisance, I rang up the Zoo and asked them to take it away to feed the lions who might be getting short of food, which they gratefully did.[26]

British troops from England had landed at Kingstown. Mrs Norway heard that . . .

. . . they are amazed at their reception, as they had been told that they were going to quell a rebellion in Ireland, and lo! on their arrival at Kingstown the whole population turned out to cheer them, giving them food, cigarettes, chocolate, and everything the hospitable inhabitants could provide, so that the puzzled troops asked plaintively: 'Who then are we going to fight, and where is the rebellion?'[35]

On marching into Dublin on Wednesday morning they met the enemy in the Mount Street Bridge area. Exposed to crossfire from snipers, the British Forces suffered their heaviest casualties of the week in this engagement, witnessed by L. G. Redmond-Howard:

The Sinn Feiners had got Clanwilliam House – a corner residence – wonderfully barricaded, and the Sherwood Foresters, who had just taken Carisbrook House and Ballsbridge after considerable losses, were now advancing to cross over the canal and so enter the town and relieve the O.D.T. in Trinity.

Clanwilliam House not only dominated the bridge, but along the whole of Northumberland Road. Along this road the troops had to pass, and they crouched down in long rows of heads – like great khaki caterpillars – in a most terribly exposed order, so that if the rebel shot failed to hit the first head it was bound to hit the second head, provided the rifle was anywhere in the vertical line. For the most part the soldiers were boys in their early twenties, utterly ignorant of the district, with orders to take the town, which was reported in the hands of a body of men whose very name was a mysterious puzzle in pronunciation, and not an enemy in sight, only a mass of civilian spectators up to within fifty yards of them and directly in front, blocking the street – the rebel enemy meanwhile inside private houses to the right and left of the narrow bridgehead, they knew not where.

I arrived on the scene a few minutes after the start of the engagement, but already one could see the poor fellows writhing in agony in the roadway, where the advanced line had been sniped by the terrible leaden bullets of the Sinn Feiners.

For half-an-hour or so I was a passive spectator, though intensely interested by the sight of a real battle going on right under my very eyes at a distance hardly more than that of the gallery from a large music-hall stage; but suddenly I felt a complete change come over me, which I yet fail to explain to myself. The usual cowardice of the spectator seemed to leave me, and I wanted to rush over and help, but I was assured that it would mean instant death to come within the line of combatants. 'The Sinn Feiners would fire on anyone, the blackguards.' This I refused to believe, and spoke to a Methodist clergyman, who soon shared my views, and together we made our way to Dun's Hospital, where the doctors and nurses in white stood in the doorway. Within a couple of minutes' conversation we had all spontaneously decided to venture under the Red Cross and put it to the test. They gave me the white coat of an ambulance-worker, and within five minutes we were all on the bridge together.

Anticipating us all, however, were two little girls of sixteen and seventeen – Kathleen Pierce and Loo Nolan by name – who rushed out of the throng with water in a jug for one of the wounded Tommies who were lying across the bridge bleeding. A great shout went up from the crowd as they saw this, and both combatants ceased firing, and, after having given the soldiers a drink, they came back amidst the cheers of soldiers, crowd, and Sinn Feiners alike . . . In little over an hour we brought in about seventy poor fellows, who lay about all along the road and canal banks, heavy packs upon their backs.

At last, however, when we had cleared the road of wounded, about dusk, there came a shout from Captain Mellville: 'Now, lads, up and all together!' Immediately there was a simultaneous rush across the bridge – a tactic which should have been adopted from the very first – some dropped, but the numbers were too many for the handful of snipers. We moved aside to give them room, and the next moment the bombers were in the garden of Clanwilliam House – one poor fellow falling and blowing the top of his head off at the gate with his own grenade. There was a 'Crash! crash! crash!' as the windows burst with the concussion, and within a few seconds the sky was lit up with the flare of the burning houses and the air rent with the screams of the Sinn Feiners as they faced cold steel. It was a ghastly scene! The smell of roasting flesh was still around the blazing buildings at ten o'clock, when we brought in the last of the dead – some of them mere boys of thirteen – and laid them out in dread rows like a Raemaeker cartoon.[40]

In the fortress-like G.P.O., Desmond Ryan had time for reflection.

I stood within it all, and a curious cloud fell over my mind and spirits, and a conflict sharpened in my mind. My old Socialist-pacifist hatred of war, my doubts about the jingoism and race-hatred of Sinn Fein, and then the spell of Pearse. A working man spoke to me and voiced my thoughts. I knew him slightly, a pale-faced man who wrote simple verse in Larkin's paper and the mosquito Press of Sinn Fein. He waved his shotgun towards Connolly and said: 'Things are desperate when an anti-militarist like him leads us into this.' Upstairs a woman echoed the conflict in my mind, for I could see a glory and a horror in all I saw, a deep respect in the heart for all those women and men behind the flames and exposed to the bullets. Half the Dublin I knew seemed there. Sometimes a messenger came to tell us: 'This is the only cheerful place in Dublin. In the city they think that you are all dead men. Black gloom down there.' Upstairs this woman spoke, half to herself, half to a poet dangling a revolver: 'Do you know that even if the British broke in I don't know whether it is right to take life. It's all right for the Volunteers. They can obey their orders.'[42]

THURSDAY 27 APRIL

Brian O'Higgins recalled the gloom that fell on the garrison at the G.P.O. when Commandant James Connolly was wounded . . .

. . . as he dispatched a squad of men to do some job of work in

Abbey Street. In his green uniform of the Citizen Army, with wide hat turned up at one side, he made a conspicuous figure, and venturing too far into the street he was picked off by a sniper. But first – and all through in fact – he made light of his wound [*a shattered ankle*], but those who were near him say he must have suffered terribly. They wanted to keep him in hospital, but whenever the alarm of an expected attack was given he insisted upon being carried down to the front door, where the fighting would be fiercest and where he could urge on his men to the last. . . .

Up to Thursday the Headquarters Staff in the G.P.O. were able to send and receive messages from most of the other positions, but on Thursday the enemy cordon, finding courage in augmented numbers, crept in closer to us, and communication even with Commandant Daly at the Four Courts became impossible. Thursday night stands out in my memory above all the rest of the week. On that night the opposite side of O'Connell Street, from Cathedral Street to O'Connell Bridge, was completely at the mercy of the fire, and we could actually feel the heat in the Post Office, while the smoke and sparks were blown to us across the wide street. I was on duty throughout the night, and I shall never forget the weird and terrible scene. All about the place – on shelves, on tables, on the floor – men who were temporarily off duty slept as soundly as if they were home in bed, each man wrapped in a blanket or overcoat and his gun by his side, ready to be grasped at the first call to arms. Five or six of our men were in the Imperial Hotel and in some of the other houses near it, and when we saw the whole place one long high sheet of flame we feared they had been caught in some of the upper rooms and burned to death. About two o'clock a.m. came a shout out of the very heart of the flames, it seemed to those who listened: 'Open the door! Open the door!' It was repeated a couple of times, and it rang from end to end of the deserted street. It was answered from our windows with 'All right; come on!' and then a stooping figure came running across the street which was as bright as at noonday. The figure was seen by the enemy at O'Connell Bridge, and immediately there was a fusillade that swept the street from sidewalk to sidewalk. It was kept up for half an hour, but in spite of it every one of the men who attempted to do so got safely across, and I tell you when the last man got inside the door there was a cheer that made the sleepers jump to their feet, certain that the attack had come at last. Then, 'The Soldier's Song' and 'The Dawning of the Day' were sung defiantly by the men at the windows, and the gloom that had been settling down upon us vanished, though we felt the end was near.

It is as he appeared that night that Pearse always comes before my mind. He was sitting to the left of the main entrance door – a position he hardly left for half an hour the whole week – a greatcoat thrown loosely over his shoulders, just as he might have sat in one of the classrooms at Sgoil Eanna when the day's work was done....[39]

It was about this time that Pearse revealed some of his most confidential thoughts to Desmond Ryan.

On the worst night of all, when the fires glared in on the ground floor of the G.P.O., Pearse came and sat beside me. He was seated on a barrel, his slightly flushed face crowned by his turned-up military hat. He watched the flames leaping and turning fantastically in the stillness, broken periodically by rifle volleys. Around him men slept on the floor, Connolly amongst them. Others were on guard behind loopholed sandbags. We talked casually for some time, bullets frightened us all, said Pearse, only liars were not afraid of bullets, we might all come through, perhaps, perhaps not. I shrugged my shoulders, I was past feeling, and told Pearse I had only one reason for wishing to survive, that I might write a book. He smiled and he sat silent, for in that great agony how futile seemed all ink and pen and words. The volleys rolled away, and Pearse watched the flames. 'All the boys were safe,' he said, with a sigh of relief. Then he suddenly turned and asked me, casually but with a certain abruptness: 'It was the right thing to do, wasn't it?' 'Yes.' 'Failure means the end of everything, the Volunteers, Ireland, all!' and the tone showed the agony of his mind, but an agony flaming to final conviction. Outside the flames grew brighter and there was a terrific burst of gunfire away in the darkness. Pearse paused and continued with deep enthusiasm and passionate conviction in his words: 'Well, *when* we are all *wiped out*, people will blame us for everything, condemn us, but only for this protest the war would have ended and nothing would have been done. After a few years, they will see the meaning of what we tried to do.' Then the conversation turned on the heroism of the insurgents: 'What a man,' said Pearse, 'what a great man is O'Rahilly, coming in here to us although he is against the Rising! . . . Emmet's two-hour Rising is nothing to this! . . . They will talk of Dublin in future as one of the splendid cities like they speak today of Paris! Dublin's name will be glorious forever! . . .'[42]

By then the artillery shelling had wrecked a considerable part of the centre of Dublin, and many buildings were on fire.

That night, with the wife of the hotel manager, Mrs Norway viewed the conflagration from a high window.

It was the most awe-inspiring sight I have ever seen. It seemed as if the whole city was on fire, the glow extending right across the heavens, and the red glare hundreds of feet high, while above the roar of the fires the whole air seemed vibrating with the noise of the great guns and machine-guns. It was an inferno! We remained spellbound . . . H. came and told us no one was to look out of the window as there was cross-firing from the United Services Club and another building, and Mr O'B., who was watching the fires from his window, had a bullet a few inches from his head!

About two a.m. I awoke to find the room illuminated in spite of dark blinds and curtains, and I rushed to the window and saw an enormous fire; it seemed to be in the direction of the Four Courts, which is in the hands of the Sinn Feiners . . .[35]

The blaze Mrs Norway saw was, in fact, the Linenhall Barracks. Earlier on Thursday she had watched the mob loot shops.

. . . clearing the great provision shops and others. From the back of this hotel you look down on an alley that connects with Grafton Street – and at the corner, the shop front in Grafton Street, but with a side entrance into this lane, is a very large and high-class fruiterer. From the windows we watched the proceedings, and I never saw anything so brazen! The mob were chiefly women and children, with a sprinkling of men. They swarmed in and out of the side door bearing huge consignments of bananas, the great bunches on the stalk, to which the children attached a cord and ran away dragging it along. Other boys had big orange boxes which they filled with tinned and bottled fruits. Women with their skirts held up received showers of apples and oranges and all kinds of fruit which were thrown from the upper windows by their pals; and ankle-deep on the ground lay all the pink and white and silver paper and paper shavings used for packing choice fruits. It was an amazing sight, and nothing daunted these people. Higher up at another shop we were told a woman was hanging out of a window dropping down loot to a friend, when she was shot through the head by a sniper.... The body dropped into the street and the mob cleared. In a few minutes a hand-cart appeared and gathered up the body, and instantly all the mob swarmed back to continue the joyful proceedings![35]

Of what St John Ervine called 'the Great Fire of Dublin', he wrote in an American magazine:

I stood at the window of my bedroom and looked at a sky that was scarlet with flames. The whole of O'Connell Street and many of the contiguous streets were like a furnace, roaring and rattling as roofs fell in a whirlpool of sparks that splashed high in the air. The finest street in Europe was consumed in a night.[21]

FRIDAY 28 APRIL

The G.P.O. in Sackville Street was ablaze, and the flames forced out the men occupying the building since Monday afternoon. Brian O'Higgins tells of the fire and the evacuation:

On Friday morning the bombardment started in real earnest, and the great strong building trembled as each immense shell burst against its walls. The men on the roof held on to their position until the flames of the bursting petrol shells drove them from it at last, and the wonder was that they had only a couple of casualties.... I was roused from a sound sleep about five o'clock that afternoon, and when I opened my eyes a comrade was standing over me. 'Get off your shelf,' he said, 'or you'll be left behind.' I got off the shelf in double quick time. 'Are we clearing out?' I asked. 'We must either clear out or be burned out,' he answered. 'Look up at the roof.' I looked up and saw what appeared to be a sea of fire rolling from side to side of the thick glass roof, with tongues of flame bursting in here and there in eager hungry fashion. The enemy had flung petrol shells on to the roof, and our men, in trying to quench the flames with a water-hose, only succeeded in spreading them all over the building, which was now doomed. The men were being called from all the positions except the windows, and lined up near the side entrance opening out into Henry Street, while hand-grenades (we had hundreds of them) and other war material that we couldn't bring with us were being carried down into the cellars, or as far away as possible from the fire. The flames burst in just beside the room in which the grenades had been stored underneath, and there was an immediate call for men to remove them before they should blow us all into the air. I shouted myself hoarse calling for men as I stood on the stairs holding a candle for The O'Rahilly, who played the hose on the invading flames until every bomb was removed. When the building was about to be evacuated The O'Rahilly, who had worked like a giant during the week, called for twelve men with rifles and bayonets to accompany him as an advance guard. The object was, I believe, to endeavour to cut our way through the intervening streets, join up with Commandant Daly at the Four Courts, if possible, and make a bid for the open country. 'It will be either a glorious victory or a glorious death, boys,' said The O'Rahilly, as he turned to his men at the door. . . .

We took with us all that we could conveniently carry of food and ammunition, and then one by one rushed in rapid succession from the side entrance, across Henry Street into Henry Place, through a veritable rain of fire from an enemy barricade either at Liffey Street or Capel Street, but very few were hit, and we proceeded up Henry Place to the head of Moore Lane. Here we were assailed by a fierce fire that seemed to come from three directions – from a barricade at the junction of Moore Lane and Parnell Street, from the roof of the Rotunda Hospital, and from the spire of Findlater's Church. The marksmanship was very bad, the bullets hitting the wall of the house at the corner so high up that by stooping we were able to dash across the danger point almost unharmed, though a few were wounded and one man was killed.

We made our way as far as Moore Street, and occupied a mineral-water stores, and a number of shops and private houses. After a time the enemy fire ceased, and they made no attempt to come to close quarters; so we fortified our new positions as best we could, and the order being absolute silence and no light, we settled down to await the coming of the last fateful day.

During the night holes were bored in the walls of several houses and a passage was made towards Parnell Street, with the object of making a dash through the enemy's lines on Saturday, and it was only when this was found to be an impossible task, I believe, that our leaders decided to surrender.[39]

On the eve of surrender Pearse issued the following manifesto:
Headquarters Army of the Irish Republic,
General Post Office, Dublin,
28th April, 1916, 9.30 a.m.

The Forces of the Irish Republic, which was proclaimed in Dublin, on Easter Monday, 24th April, have been in possession of the central part of the capital, since 12 noon on that day. Up to yesterday afternoon Headquarters was in touch with all the main outlying positions, and, despite furious, and almost continuous assaults by the British Forces, all those positions were still being held, and the Commandants in charge were confident of their ability to hold them for a long time.

During the course of yesterday afternoon, and evening, the enemy succeeded in cutting our communications with our other positions in the city, and Headquarters is today isolated.

The enemy has burnt down whole blocks of houses, apparently with the object of giving themselves a clear field for the play of artillery and field guns against us. We have been bombarded during the evening and night by shrapnel and machine-gun fire, but without material damage to our position, which is of great strength.

We are busy completing arrangements for the final defence of Headquarters, and are determined to hold it while the buildings last.

I desire now, lest I may not have an opportunity later, to pay homage to the gallantry of the soldiers of Irish Freedom who have during the past few days been writing with fire and steel the most glorious chapter in the later history of Ireland. Justice can never be done to their heroism, to their discipline, to their gay and unconquerable spirit in the midst of peril and death.

Let me, who have led them into this, speak in my own, and in my fellow-commanders' names, and in the name of Ireland present and to come, their praise, and ask those who come after them to remember them.

For four days they have fought and toiled, almost without cessation, almost without sleep, and in the intervals of fighting they have sung songs of the freedom of Ireland. No man has complained, no man has asked 'Why?' Each individual has spent himself, happy to pour out his strength for Ireland and for freedom. If they do not win this fight, they will at least have deserved to win it. But win it they will, although they may win it in death. Already they have won a great thing. They have redeemed Dublin from any shame, and made her name splendid among the names of cities.

If I were to mention names of individuals, my list would be a long one.

I will name only that of Commandant General James Connolly, Commanding the Dublin Division. He lies wounded, but is still the guiding brain of our resistance.

If we accomplish no more than we have accomplished, I am satisfied. I am satisfied that we have saved Ireland's honour. I am satisfied that we should have accomplished more, that we should have accomplished the task of enthroning, as well as proclaiming, the Irish Republic as a Sovereign State, and our arrangements for a simultaneous rising of the whole country, with a combined plan as sound as the Dublin plan has been proved to be, had been allowed to go through on Easter Sunday. Of the fatal countermanding order which prevented those plans from being carried out, I shall not speak further. Both Eoin MacNeill and we have acted in the best interests of Ireland.

For my part, as to anything I have done in this, I am not afraid to face either the judgment of God, or the judgment of posterity.

P. H. Pearse
Commandant General,
Commanding in Chief the Army of the Irish Republic and President of the Provisional Government.[43]

Forty of the Cumann na mBan (League of Women) were attached to rebel headquarters at the G.P.O. and the main body stayed there from Easter Monday until ordered to leave by Commandant Pearse on the following Friday. Three women stayed on to look after wounded insurgents: Julia Grenan, Winifred Carney, and Elizabeth O'Farrell. Here is the last-named's account of the evacuation of the G.P.O.

On Thursday afternoon it became evident that the G.P.O. could not be much longer held. The members of the Cumann na mBhan, with three exceptions, left by Commandant Pearse's orders. . . . About eight o'clock on Friday evening, April 28th, 1916, the building being entirely in flames, we retreated from there under very heavy fire, the intention as I understood being to cut our way through at some point and to join up with Commandant Daly at the Four Courts.

Evacuation of G.P.O. – We left by a side entrance in Henry Street, crossed to Henry Place and around into Moore Lane. There was a barricade erected midway in Moore Lane, and it was very dangerous passing it, as the military were firing over it. We left in three sections, I being in the last. Com. Pearse was the last to leave the building. He went round to see that no one was left behind. We immediately preceded him, bullets raining from all quarters as we rushed to Moore Lane. As I passed the barricade I tripped and fell; in a second some man rushed out of the house on the corner of Moore Lane and Moore Street (Gogan's), where the second section had taken cover, took me up in his arms and rushed back to the house. It was Sean McGarry, of Ballybough Road . . . When I entered the parlour of the house I found some of the members of the Provisional Government already there, the house well barricaded, and James Connolly lying on a stretcher in the middle of the room. I went over to him and asked him how he felt, he answered 'Bad,' and remarked 'The soldier who wounded me did a good day's work for the British Government.' After a short time the other members of the Provisional Government came in. Some mattresses were then procured, on which we placed Mr Connolly, and other wounded men. There were seventeen wounded in the retreat from the G.P.O. and I spent the night (April 28th) helping to nurse them. Around us we could hear the roar of burning buildings, machine-guns playing on the houses, and at intervals what seemed to be hand-grenades.

Easter Week 1916 155

SATURDAY 29 APRIL

The morning of the 29th I spent in helping to cook for the other Volunteers who had worked hard through the night burrowing from house to house up towards the top of Moore Street. After breakfast, Mr Connolly and the other wounded men were carried through the holes, and all others followed. Mr Connolly was put to bed in a back room in 16 Moore Street. The members of the Provisional Government were in this room for a considerable length of time (P. H. Pearse, J. Connolly, J. Plunkett, T. J. Clarke, and Sean McDermott), where they held a council of war. Willie Pearse was also with them. On the floor of the room lay three wounded Volunteers and a soldier, a prisoner, who was badly injured, lay on a bed on the side of the room. Winifred Carney, Julia Grenan, and I came in to attend them. The soldier asked us would Pearse speak to him. Pearse said, 'Certainly.' The soldier then asked Pearse to lift him a little in the bed. Pearse did this, the soldier putting his arms round his neck. This was all. Pearse returned to James Connolly's bedside, and a consultation was continued in private.[38]

Brian O'Higgins concludes:

My special work came to an end when we left the Post Office, and so on Saturday morning I found myself helping to take wounded through the passage made during the night, to a shed in the mineral-water stores. At least we succeeded in getting them through, and placed them on some dry straw in an open shed, where they were made as comfortable as they could be with serious wounds that were only roughly bandaged, because most of the hospital supplies had to be left behind in the sudden retreat from the Post Office. The young doctor who was with us, and who was deported as a common 'rebel' afterwards (Dr Jim Ryan, T.D.) did all he could with the appliances at hand and went from man to man of the wounded all through that night and that day, and but for his untiring care many would surely have succumbed to their wounds. Three members of the Cumann na mBhan – Miss Carney, Miss Grenan, and Miss O'Farrell – who had insisted on staying on to help the wounded when their comrades were sent out to Jervis Street Hospital on Thursday evening, worked unceasingly throughout Friday night and on Saturday preparing what food there was for the wounded men, and doing all that could be done under the circumstances to relieve their sufferings.

There was practically no food in Moore Street, everybody was fatigued and hungry, some were weak and ill, but there was no grumbling, and all were ready to go out at the first word of command and sell their lives as dearly as possible in the barricaded streets.

It was a beautiful day, the sun shone down upon us from a cloudless sky and there was hardly a breeze. As we lay there in that shed in Moore Street in dead silence – for we were quite close to an enemy barricade – thoughts came that had been kept afar during the previous days of strenuous toil – thoughts of those who were waiting and praying for us at home, thoughts of those who had fallen in the fight, thoughts of the wounded men by our side and of our inability to relieve their pain – and for the first time during that glorious week we felt sad and depressed. Now and then a shot rang out and a bullet sang dismally over our heads; birds fluttered by us terrified at the unusual scene, a couple of horses loosed by us from a burning stable the evening before wandered up and down a nearby lane, and always we heard the roaring and crackling and hissing of the flames from which we had fled, and every moment they seemed to draw nearer and nearer. Death was in the air that day and we waited for its coming.

Then late in the afternoon came the unexpected news that terms of some sort had been arranged between our leaders and the enemy...[39]

Padraic Pearse called on Elizabeth O'Farrell to carry a message to the British Commander in order to negotiate terms of peace. For two days she carried messages between General Lowe of the British Army and the commanders at the centres of rebel resistance. Her narrative of the surrender, printed in the Catholic Bulletin, *is one of the most interesting recollections of the 1916 Rising.*

Message to General Lowe – ... I got orders from Sean McDermott to provide a white flag – he first hung one out of the house to ensure me from being fired on. I left by the house (Gorman's), 15 Moore Street, about 12.45 p.m. on Saturday the 29th, with a verbal message from Commandant Pearse to the Commander of the British

Forces, to the effect that he wished to treat with them. I waved the small white flag which I carried and the military ceased firing and called me up to the barrier which was across the top of Moore Street into Parnell Street. As I passed up Moore Street I saw, at the corner of Sackville Lane, The O'Rahilly's hat and a revolver lying on the ground – I thought he had gone into some house. I gave my message to the officer in charge, and he asked me how many girls were down there. I said three. He said, 'Take my advice and go down again and bring the other two girls out of it.' He was about putting me back again through the barrier when he changed his mind and said, 'However, you had better wait, I suppose this will have to be reported'. Then he sent another officer with me up Parnell Street, towards the Parnell statue – he sent into one of the houses there (I think it was 70 or 71 Parnell Street) for someone in command. The Officer in Command then came out.

I said: 'The Commandant of the Irish Republican Army wishes to treat with the Commandant of the British Forces in Ireland.'

Officer: 'The Irish Republican Army – the Sinn Feiners you mean.'

I replied: 'The Irish Republican Army they call themselves, and I think that a very good name, too.'

Officer: 'Will Pearse be able to be moved on a stretcher?'

I said: 'Commandant Pearse doesn't need a stretcher.'

Officer: 'Pearse does need a stretcher, Madam.'

I again answered: 'Commandant Pearse doesn't need a stretcher.'

To another officer: 'Take that Red Cross off her and bring her over there and search her – she is a spy.'

The officer, as ordered, proceeded to cut the Red Cross off my arm, also off the front of my apron, and then took me over to the hall of the National Bank on the corner of Parnell Street and Cavendish Row, where he searched me and found two pairs of scissors (one of which he afterwards returned to me), some sweets, bread, and cakes, etc. Being satisfied that I wasn't dangerous he then took me (of all places in the world) to Tom Clarke's shop as a prisoner – all this procedure occupied about three-quarters of an hour. I was kept in the shop for about another three-quarters of an hour, when another military man came in – whom I learned was Brigadier General Lowe. He treated me in a very gentlemanly manner. I gave Gen. Lowe my message and he said he would take me in a motor-car to the top of Moore Street, and that I was to go back to Mr Pearse and tell him that Gen. Lowe would not treat at all until he (Mr Pearse) would surrender unconditionally,' and that I must be back in half an hour, as hostilities must go on. Then the officer whom I first interviewed wrote a note to this effect for Gen. Lowe. They both came with me in the motor to Moore Street. It was then about 2.25 p.m. I went on to 16 Moore Street, and as I passed Sackville Lane, the first turn on the left in Moore Street going down from Parnell Street, I looked up and saw the dead body of The O'Rahilly lying about four yards up the Lane . . . I gave both the verbal and written message to Com. Pearse, and told him I was to be back in half an hour. The situation was discussed, and I was sent back with a written message. I went back again to the top of Moore Street, where General Lowe was waiting for me in the motor-car. . . . Whatever was in the note from Com. Pearse to Gen. Lowe I cannot say; but, Gen. Lowe's reply to it was: 'Go back and tell Mr Pearse that I will not treat at all unless he surrenders unconditionally and that Mr Connolly follows on a stretcher.' (Here Gen. Lowe apologized to me and said, 'It is Connolly that is wounded, not Pearse'.) He told me then that unless Mr Pearse and I came back in half an hour he would begin hostilities again. I brought back that message. The members of the Provisional Government having held a short council, Com. Pearse decided to accompany me back to Gen. Lowe.

Commandant Pearse surrenders – It was about 3.30 p.m. when Gen. Lowe received Com. Pearse at the top of Moore Street, in Parnell Street. One of the officers that had been a prisoner in the G.P.O. was asked to identify Com. Pearse and he could not – he said he did not see him in the G.P.O. He asked Com. Pearse was he in the G.P.O. and he said he was – the officer said, 'I did not see you there.' Com. Pearse then handed up his sword to Gen. Lowe.

Gen. Lowe to Com. Pearse: 'The only condition I make is that I will allow the other Commandants to surrender. I understand you have the Countess de Markievicz down there.'

Com. Pearse: 'No, she is not with me.'
Gen. Lowe: 'Oh, I know she is down there.'
Com. Pearse: 'Don't accuse me of speaking an untruth.'
Gen. Lowe: 'Oh, I beg your pardon, Mr. Pearse, but I know she is in the area.'
Com. Pearse: 'Well, she is not with me, sir.'
Gen. Lowe then suggested that the military should detain me for the night in order to take around next day Com. Pearse's order to surrender to the other Commandants, when Com. Pearse would give me a list of the addresses of the occupations by the Irish Republican troops, promising, at the same time, to set me free and give me a safe convoy pass when I should have accomplished this. Com. Pearse turned to me and said: 'Will you agree to this?' I said: 'Yes, if you wish it.' He said: 'I do wish it.' Pearse then shook hands with me but spoke no words. After this he was taken away in a motor-car, down O'Connell Street, accompanied by Gen. Lowe's son and another officer inside, and an armed guard on the footboard outside. He was preceded in another car by Gen. Lowe and Capt. Wheeler. I saw him no more. [38]

Elizabeth O'Farrell carried Pearse's surrender to the other Commandants. The typewritten surrender was signed by P. H. Pearse, and agreement to its conditions added by James Connolly and Thomas MacDonagh.

In order to prevent the further slaughter of Dublin citizens, and in the hope of saving the lives of our followers now surrounded and hopelessly outnumbered, the members of the Provisional Government present at Headquarters have agreed to an unconditional surrender, and the Commandants of the various districts in the City and Country will order their commands to lay down arms.

P. H. Pearse
29th April 1916
3.45 p.m.

I agree to these conditions for the men only under my own

command in the Moore Street District and for the men in the Stephen's Green Command.

James Connolly
April 29 '16

On consultation with Commandant Ceannt and other officers I have decided to agree to unconditional surrender also.

Thomas MacDonagh[43]

Julia Grenan also wrote of her experiences for the Catholic Bulletin: *In Sackville (O'Connell) Street, outside the Gresham Hotel* . . .

The Volunteers laid down their arms and equipment, and our Ambulance Corps were ordered to take off their Red Crosses. Two officers came down and one said to the other: 'There's Tom Clarke.' One of them called Mr Clarke out of line and several other officers came 'to have a look at him'. Another officer looking at Sean MacDermott said, 'You have cripples in your army?', and Sean replied, 'You have your place, sir, and I have mine, and you had better mind your place, sir.' . . . We were then marched up O'Connell Street to the plot of grass outside the Rotunda, and we were put sitting here in a space which would have seated about 150. As, with the Four Courts' men, there were four hundred confined here, we were very uncomfortable. It was night now and very cold. Sean MacDermott, who was in bad health, and Joseph Plunkett, who had been recently ill, suffered intensely from the cold. Miss Carney spread her own coat and Commandant Connolly's coat (which he had given her) on the grass and insisted on Sean MacDermott and Joseph Plunkett having a little warmth and rest. . . . About nine a.m. we were ordered to march to O'Connell Street. Miss Carney and I waited to assist Sean MacDermott. He explained to the officer in charge that he was unable to march, so he was placed alone under escort. We were placed at the rear of the main body, and marched up to Richmond Barracks. About three-quarters of an hour after our arrival Sean MacDermott arrived completely worn out from the night's exposure and the fatiguing march, and pale as death. Joseph Plunkett fainted on his arrival and we saw him being carried in. Miss Carney and I were then taken off the ranks, and given in charge to an officer, who treated us courteously. He provided us with tea.... We then marched straight to Kilmainham Jail. It was quite dark by this time. The jail is gloomy, and the soldiers going round with flickering candles only added to the general depression.... At dawn on Wednesday, May 3rd, we were awakened by the volleys that executed Pearse, Clarke, and MacDonagh.... Morning after morning we were awake praying, and listening for the volleys, and four times we heard them. At first the wardress said it was distant fighting. But we knew the truth. I spent ten days in Kilmainham and was released with a number of the Cumann na mBhan on Tuesday, May 9th.[24]

The official list of casualties was published on *11 May*.

	Killed	Wounded	Missing	Total
Military officers	17	46	–	63
Military, other ranks	86	311	9	406
Royal Irish Constabulary, officers	2	—	–	2
Royal Irish Constabulary, other ranks	12	23	–	35
Dublin Metropolitan Police	3	3	–	6
Civilians and insurgents	180	614	–	794
	300	997	9	1,306

As many of the rebels wore no uniform, their casualties were included with those of civilians.

The confusion of orders had led to only a few scattered risings of a minor nature in the country outside of Dublin. In a revival of the spirit of 1798, Enniscorthy was held by local Volunteers from Thursday to Saturday of Easter Week, and 600 rebels surrendered on Vinegar Hill, scene of the great rebel camp of 1798. But there had been no actual fighting. Most insurgent activity was in Galway, where Liam Mellows, a Sinn Fein organizer who had been deported a few weeks before, returned to lead about a thousand men, poorly armed, some carrying only pikes like the men of 1798. They were shelled by a warship in Galway Bay, and dispersed after learning of Pearse's surrender in Dublin.

There were some raids on police barracks in County Louth and County Meath. The north stayed quiet.

'How deep in Irish hearts lies this passion for insurrection,' Augustine Birrell wrote to Asquith on 29 April, and two days later the Prime Minister accepted the Chief Secretary's resignation. Birrell had hoped to usher in Home Rule, which several Liberal Governments had worked towards. Now he felt 'smashed to pieces'. Sir Matthew Nathan resigned on 3 May. Birrell had some words of comfort for his Under-Secretary: 'Better to sink with some people than to go to the House of Lords with others.'

General Sir John Maxwell, who had arrived in Dublin on 28 April to take up duties as the new Commander-in-Chief of the British Forces in Ireland, had the responsibility for punishing the rebels. Swiftly, courts martial were held in secret and fourteen of the Dublin leaders were executed, including the seven signatories of the Proclamation of the Republic. The last executions were on 12 May, with the deaths of James Connolly and Sean MacDermott. Connolly, in pain, sat on a chair to be shot. Nora Connolly spoke to the priest who had been with her father during his last moments.

'I was sure there would be no more executions. The ambulance that brought you home came for me. I felt so sure that I would not be needed that for the first time I locked the doors. I was astounded.'

'But how did they shoot him?'

'The ambulance brought me to your father. He was a wonderful man. I'm sorry to say that of all the men that were executed he was the only one I did not know personally. I will always thank God as long as I live that He permitted me to be with your father till he was dead.'

'Yes, Father; yes. But they shot him. How – ?'

'They carried him from his bed in a stretcher to an ambulance and drove him to Kilmainham Jail. They carried the stretcher from the ambulance to the jail yard. They put him in a chair. . . . He was very brave and cool. . . . I asked him: 'Will you pray for the men who are about to shoot you?' And he answered: 'I will say a prayer for all brave men who do their duty.' . . . And then they shot him. . . .'[37]

There was one further execution. Sir Roger Casement was found guilty of high treason and hanged on 3 August. Two controversial aspects of the case were firstly that the prosecutor was F. E. Smith, who had been involved with Sir Edward Carson in armed opposition to the Crown two years before, and secondly that copies of what were said to be extracts from Casement's diaries, which showed him to be a promiscuously practising homosexual, were circulated among influential people pressing for a reprieve. Casement's remains were taken from London to Ireland for reburial in 1966. The 'black diaries' are in the Public Records Office in London.

Pearse and Connolly had known that defeat for the rebellion was certain ('We are all going to be slaughtered,' Connolly told a friend on Easter Monday morning); yet each in his own way, one mystical and the other realistic, divined that the blood-sacrifice of Easter Week would awaken the national soul and activate the final drive for Irish independence, which came in less than six years. 1916 saw the culmination of what Dr Brian Inglis has called the 'patriot myth', using the latter word 'Irish-fashion to describe a body of emotion that has far more power over the destinies of a nation than the promptings of reason or self-interest'. (The Story of Ireland, Faber, 1966.) The quality of the rebels of 1916, not least in their freedom from religious hatreds and sectarian violence of the kind that marred earlier rebellions, made them the true heirs of Tone and Emmet – and this contributed in large measure to the flowering of the 'myth'. St John Ervine, himself a Belfast Protestant, put it like this:

One thinks of three big rebellions in Ireland and of their failures. The first failed because there were no leaders good enough for the followers they had; the second failed because the followers were not good enough for the leaders they had. In this third rebellion leaders and followers were worthy of one another, matchless in spirit and devotion. But they had not the people behind them, and they had to fight an immeasurably superior force.[21]

Suddenly, in the words of W. B. Yeats, 'a terrible beauty was born,' and all was 'changed, changed utterly'. The rebel prisoners had gone to jail mocked and execrated; but they came out, in December 1916 and June 1917, as heroes to the majority of the Irish people.

Among the disparaged patriots of Easter Week were William Cosgrave

(*South Dublin Union*), who became Prime Minister of the Irish Free State; Michael Collins (*G.P.O.*), who became Commander-in-Chief of the Free State Army; and Eamon de Valera (*Boland's Mill*), who became Prime Minister of the twenty-six counties republic and in 1959 its President. And a marching song the Easter rebels sang became the national anthem of an independent Ireland.

> Soldiers are we, whose lives are pledged to Ireland,
> Some have come from a land beyond the wave,
> Sworn to be free, no more our ancient sireland
> Shall shelter the despot or the slave. . . .

It is often suggested that the execution of Pearse, Connolly, and other rebel leaders turned the tide of Irish public opinion from condemning the insurgents to venerating them as martyrs and supporting their ideals. It seems problematic that this in itself would be enough to effect so remarkable a change. National consciousness, as we have seen, was already growing, and would probably have found expression following the rebellion, even if the leaders had lived. Whatever the reason, public support moved away from the Irish Party led by Redmond to the more extreme Sinn Fein. In the postwar general election of December 1918 Sinn Fein won 73 out of 105 seats for all Ireland. Instead of taking their seats at Westminster the Sinn Feiners set up an Irish Republican Parliament, Dail Eireann, meeting on 21 January 1919 and ratifying the Republic proclaimed in 1916. The following two-and-a-half years were taken up with guerilla warfare by the Irish Republican Army against the British Army and the Royal Irish Constabulary, which was augmented by a force of recruits from England whose uniforms gave them the name 'Black-and-Tans'. The crudity and toughness with which the latter set about their task further pushed Irish public opinion behind the republicans.

The Anglo-Irish Treaty was signed on 6 December 1921, whereby twenty-six counties of Ireland became the Irish Free State, with their own parliament in Dublin, though there would be an oath of allegiance to the Crown and certain arrangements whereby Britain would have use of the main Irish ports. Six of the nine counties of Ulster became Northern Ireland, linked with Britain, but having a parliament in

Belfast, officially opened by King George V. To out-and-out republicans the signing of the treaty was an act of treachery to the principles of Tone and Emmet and the Martyrs of 1916. The split on the issue led to a bitter civil war between the two factions, during which more lives were lost than in the struggle against the British. Elections in June 1922 produced a parliament with a clear pro-Treaty majority. Michael Collins, who had predicted that the signing of the Treaty would be his death warrant, was shot dead in an ambush at Bealnablath, County Cork, on 22 August 1922. The Free State Government finally overcame the challenge to its authority on 24 May 1923.

The two main political parties in the Republic have their origins in the Civil War situation: Fine Gael as the party of the Free State, and Fianna Fail as the party of the anti-Treaty republicans. In the elections of 1927 de Valera's party, Fianna Fail ('Soldiers of Destiny'), won a majority in parliament and has since been the party most years in office. During the Second World War de Valera maintained Irish neutrality. The final link between the Ireland of the twenty-six counties and the British Commonwealth was not severed until 1949; at the same time the Ireland Act gave loyalists of the six counties the assurance that no constitutional change would be made without the consent of the Parliament of Northern Ireland. Following fifty years of one-party (Unionist) rule in Northern Ireland, there has been a return of sectarian killings and guerilla warfare between the I.R.A. and the British Army. In 1972 the Parliament of Northern Ireland was prorogued. At the time of writing the position remains turbulent and complex. Yet again a 'final solution' to the 'Irish question' is being sought.

Sources

1. A field officer: quoted Maxwell, W. H., *A History of the Irish Rebellion in 1798*, London, 1845.
2. A young man who fought with the rebels in County Down: quoted McComb, William, *Guide to Belfast*, Belfast, 1861.
3. Alexander, James, *Some Account of the first Apparent Symptoms of the Late Rebellion in the County of Kildare ... with a succinct narrative of Some of the Most Remarkable passages in the Rise and Progress of the Rebellion in the County of Wexford*, Dublin, 1800.
4. An artillery officer at New Ross: quoted Taylor, George, *An History of the Rise, Progress and Suppression of the Rebellion in the County of Wexford, in the year 1798*, Dublin, 1800.
5. Audley, James Lord, Earl of Castlehaven, *Memoirs, 1642–1651*, London, 1680.
6. Barbé, L.: in papers supplied by Jean Payen de la Fouleresse to Christian V of Denmark. *Notes and Queries*, July 1877.
7. Barrington, Sir Jonah, *Personal Sketches of his own Times*, 3 vols., London, 1827–32.
8. Bernard, Dr Nicholas: quoted Gardiner, S. R., *History of the Commonwealth and Protectorate, 1649–1660*, 3 vols., London, 1896–1903.
9. Birrell, Augustine, *Things Past Redress*, London, 1937.
10. Brownrigg, Mrs.: quoted Wheeler, H. F. B., and Broadley, A.M., *The War in Wexford*, London, 1910.
11. Byrne, Miles, *Memoirs*, 2 vols., Paris, 1863, and Dublin, 1906.
12. Caulfield, James: quoted Plowden, Francis, *An Historical Review of the State of Ireland, from the invasion of the country under Henry II to its Union with Great Britain*, 2 vols., London, 1801.
13. Cloney, Thomas, *A Personal Narrative of these Transactions in the County of Wexford, in which the Author was engaged, during the Awful Period of 1798*, Dublin, 1832.
14. Cornwallis, Charles, 1st Marquis, *Correspondence*, 3 vols., London, 1859.

Sources

15 Cromwell, Oliver, *Letters and Speeches*, with elucidations by Carlyle, Thomas, 2 vols., New York, 1845.
16 Cromwell, Oliver: Clarke Papers, ii, 200; quoted Gardiner, S. R., *History of the Commonwealth and Protectorate, 1649–1660*, 3 vols., London, 1896–1903.
17 Cuffe, Maurice, *A brief narrative of the beginning and continuance of the Commotion in the County of Clare, alias Thomond, against the Protestants of the said County, chiefly against the Castle of Ballyally, then defended by Maurice Cuffe, Esq. against the Rebels, from 1 November, 1641 to 15 June, 1642*. In Croker, Thomas Crofton (ed.), *Narratives illustrative of the contests in Ireland in 1641 and 1690*, Camden Society, London, MDCCCXLI.
18 Devoy, John, *Recollections of an Irish Rebel*, New York, 1929.
19 Edgar, Rev. Dr Samuel: quoted McComb, William, *Guide to Belfast*, Belfast, 1861.
20 Emmet, Robert: quoted Madden, Richard R., *The United Irishmen, their lives and times*, 7 vols., London, 1842–6.
21 Ervine, St John: *Century Magazine*, New York, November 1916.
22 Filgate, Henry P.: letter, dated 21 February 1905, to the editor of the *Gaelic American*. Quoted Devoy, John, *Recollections of an Irish Rebel*, New York, 1929.
23 Fisher, John: quoted Madden, Richard R., *The United Irishmen, their Lives and Times*, 7 vols., London, 1842–46.
24 Grenan, Julia: in *The Catholic Bulletin*, 1917.
25 Harvey, Beauchamp Bagenal: quoted Gordon, Rev. James Bentley, *History of the Rebellion in Ireland in the Year 1798*, London and Dublin, 1803.
26 Headlam, Maurice, *Irish Reminiscences*, London, 1947.
27 Holmes, George: letter, dated 16 November 1689, to William Fleming. Historical Manuscripts Commission, Twelfth Report, App. VII, pp. 264–280.
28 Hope, James: quoted Madden, Richard R., *Down and Antrim in '98*, Dublin, n.d.
29 Humbert, General Joseph Amable: proclamation, in National Library of Ireland, Dublin.

30 Jackson, Charles, *A Narrative of the Sufferings and Escapes of Charles Jackson, late resident at Wexford in Ireland*, 1798.
31 MacLaren, Archibald, *A Minute Description of the Battles of Gorey, Arklow and Vinegar Hill, together with the Movements of the Army through the Wicklow Mountains*, 1798.
32 Meagher, Thomas Francis: written in Richmond Prison, Dublin, 1849, published in the *Nation*. Quoted Gwynn, Denis, *Young Ireland in 1848*, Cork, 1949.
33 Moore, Sir John: Maurice, Maj.-General Sir J. F. (ed.), *Diary*, London, 1904.
34 Mulholland, Captain (?), a British officer serving with the regiment of Sir John Clotworthy, *The History of the War in Ireland from 1641 to 1665*, Dublin, 1873.
35 Norway, Mrs. Hamilton, *The Sinn Fein Rebellion As I Saw It*, Dublin, 1916.
36 Oath of Association used by rebels *circa* November 1641. H. M. C. Ormonde MSS., N.S., ii, 24. Quoted Clarke, J. S., *Life of James II*, 2 vols., London, 1816.
37 O'Brien, Nora Connolly, *Portrait of a Rebel Father*, London, 1935.
38 O'Farrell, Elizabeth: in *The Catholic Bulletin*, April, 1917.
39 O'Higgins, Brian, *The Soldier's Story of Easter Week*, Dublin, 1925.
40 Redmond-Howard, L. G., *Six Days of the Irish Republic*, Dublin and London, 1916.
41 Rinuccini, Giovanni Battista, *The Embassy in Ireland*, Dublin, 1873.
42 Ryan, Desmond, *Remembering Sion*, London, 1934.
43 *Sinn Fein Rebellion Handbook, Easter, 1916. Irish Times*, Dublin, 1917.
44 Stevens, John: Murray, Rev. R. H. (ed.), *Journal*, Oxford, 1912.
45 Stock, Joseph, *Narrative of What Passed at Killala during the French Invasion of 1798*, London, 1801.
46 Stoker, E. A.: quoted Redmond-Howard, L. G., *Six Days of the Irish Republic*, Dublin and London, 1916.

47 Storey, Rev. George, *Impartial History*, London, 1691.
48 Swift, Jonathan, *A Short View of the State of Ireland*, Dublin, 1728.
49 Temple, Sir John, *The Irish Rebellion*, London, 1646.
50 Thomson, James: in *Belfast Magazine*, Vol. 1, No. 1, 1825.
51 Tone, Theobald Wolfe: Tone, T. W. (ed.), *Life, written by himself and continued by his son; with his political writings and fragments of his diary*, 2 vols., Washington, 1826.
52 Walker, Rev. George: Dwyer, Philip, (ed.), *A True History of the Siege of Londonderry in 1689*, London, 1893.
53 White, Mrs: quoted *History of the Rebellion in Ireland in the year 1798*, printed by W. Borrowdale, 1806.
54 Wood, Thomas: quoted Wood, Anthony, Clark, Andrew (ed.), *The Life and Times of Anthony Wood*, 1632–95, 5 vols., Oxford, 1891–95.
55 Young, Arthur, *Tour in Ireland*, Dublin, 1780.

Index

Abbey Theatre, Dublin, 124, 129
Abercorn, Duke of, 125
Abercromby, General Sir Ralph, 67
Act of Supremacy, 6
Adrian IV, Pope, v, 3
Alexander, James, quoted, 85-88
America, 60, 61, 118, 129
Anglo-Irish Treaty (1921), 164
Anne, Queen, 57
Antrim, 99, 100
Antrim, County, 98, 99, 100
Ardee, 41
Arklow, 78, 89-91, 92, 94
Ashe, Thomas, 134
Ashton, Sir Arthur, 21
Asquith, Henry Herbert, 124, 125, 162
Athlone, 52

Ballinamuck, 109
Ballingale, 70
Ballyally, Castle of, 10
Ballyboley, 100
Ballymena, 99
Ballynahinch, 100-106
Bantry Bay, 62-64, 107
Barbé, L., quoted, 41-46

Barrington, Sir Jonah, quoted, 74-75, 97-98
Belfast, 61, 99, 125, 165
Benburb, 17, 19, 27, 116
Bernard, Dr Nicholas, quoted, 23-24
Berwick, Duke of, 40, 47
Birrell, Augustine, 136, quoted, 126, 162
'Black and Tans', 164
Boland's Mill, Dublin, 134, 164
Bonaparte, Napoleon, 64-66
Boru, Brian, 3, 116
Boulavogue, 68
Boycott, Captain, 123
Boyne, Battle of the, 35, 40, 41-47, 52, 53
Bowen-Colthurst, Capt. J. C., 140, 141
Brehon Law, 4, 5, 7
British Army, 127, 131, 156, 165
Brownrigg, Mrs, quoted, 96
Bruce, Edward, 4
Brugha, Cathal, 134
Bunclody (Newtownbarry), 78, 89
Butt, Isaac, M.P., 123
Byrne, Miles, quoted, 93-94

Camden, Lord, 61
Carlow, County, 67
Carnew, 68
Carney, Winifred, 154, 155, 160
Carson, Sir Edward, 125, 126, 163
Casement, Sir Roger, 127, 128, 133, 136, 162, 163
Castlebar, 108
Castlehaven, James Audley, Earl of, quoted, 12–14
Catholic Association (1823), 116
Catholic Bulletin, quoted, 154–155, 156–161
Catholicism, 5, 6, 9, 25
Catholics, 7, 12–14, 25, 30, 31, 35, 52, 53, 57, 58, 60, 68, 98, 113
Caulfield, Dr, Bishop of Wexford, quoted, 76
Ceannt, Eamonn, (Kent, Edmund), 130, 131, 134, 160
Charlemont, 8, 17
Charles I, King, 9, 14, 19
Charles II, King, 30, 35, 40, 57
Christian V, King, 41
Churchill, Lord Randolph, 125
Church of England, 6, 7
Church of Ireland, 123
City Hall, Dublin, 134, 136
Clanwilliam House, Dublin, 144, 145, 146
Clare Militia, 83
Clark, Sir George, quoted, 58
Clarke, Thomas J., 130, 131, 157, 160
Cloney, Thomas, quoted, 68–70, 80–84
Clonmel, 27–30
Colclough, Dr J. H., 72, 74, 97
Collins, Michael, 164, 165

Connaught, 30
Connolly, James, vi, 129, 130, 131, 132, 138, 146, 147, 153, 154, 155, 160, 162
Connolly, Sean, 134
Cook, Captain, 61
Cooke, Edward, 75
Cork, 15, 52
Cork Militia, North, 68, 69, 72
Cornwallis, Lord, quoted, 113
Cosgrave, William, 164
Covenant, Ulster, 125–126
Cranmer, Archbishop, 6
Cromwell, Oliver, v, 3, 6, 11, 24, 25, 27–30, 35; quoted 19, 20, 21–23, 26–27
Cuffe, Maurice, quoted, 10–11
Cumann na mBan (League of Women), 138, 153, 154, 161
Curragh, 126, 135, 136, 141

Daly, Ned, 134, 151
Danes, 3
Dartmouth, the, 39
Davitt, Michael, 123
Dawning of the Day, The, 148
Declaration of Independence (1782), 59
Defenders, 61, 98
De Valera, Eamon, 134, 164, 165
Devoy, John, quoted, 120
Dickson, the Rev. Steele, 100
Donegal Militia, 72
Douglas, Captain, 39
Down, County, 8, 98, 100–107
Drogheda, 11, storming, 20–25, 26
Dublin, 4, 5, 7, 8, 9, 11, 19, 21, 58, 66, 89, 119, 127, 128–165

Index

Dublin Castle, 8, 114, 127, 135, 136, 142, 143
Duffy, Charles Gavan, 116, 118
Dundalk, 20, 40
Dungannon, 60
Dunlaoghaire (see Kingstown)
Dun's Hospital, Dublin, 145

Edgar, the Rev Dr Samuel, quoted, 101–102
Edward I, King, 4
Edward III, King, 4
Elizabeth I, Queen, 6, 7
Emmet, Robert, 113–116, 149, 163, 165
Enniscorthy, 69, 92, 93, 97, 161
Enniskillen, 35, 40
Ervine, St John, quoted, 129, 131–132, 133, 140, 150, 163

Fenians, 113, 118–120
Fianna Fail, 165
Filgate, Henry P., quoted, 119–120
Fine Gael, 165
Fisher, John, quoted, 115–116
Fitzgerald, James Fitzmaurice, 6, 25
Fitzgerald, Lord Edward, 66
Fitzwilliam, Lord, 61
'Flight of the Earls', 7
'Flight of the Wild Geese', 52, 57
Flood, Henry, 59
Four Courts Dublin, 134, 149, 151
France, 35, 52, 61, 62, 98
French Revolution, 61, 73, 132

Gaelic Athletic Association, 124

Gaelic League, 124, 127
Gaels, 3
Galway, County, 13, 161
General Post Office, Dublin, 131–141
George V, King, 125, 165
Germany, 127, 128
Ginckel, General, 52
Gladstone, William Ewart, 123, 124, 125
Glamorgan, Earl of, 14, 15
Gorey, 68, 71, 78, 94
Grafton Street, Dublin, 128, 133, 149, 150
Grand Prior's Regiment, 50
Grattan, Henry, 59
Grenan, Julia, 154, 155; quoted, 160–161

Harcourt Street, Dublin, 142
Harvey, Beauchamp Bagenal, 72, 74, 75, 78, 79, 83, 97; quoted, 88
Headlam, Maurice, quoted, 142–144
Henry II, King, v, 3
Henry VII, King, 5
Henry VIII, King, 5, 6
Henry Street, Dublin, 138
Hoche, General Lazare, 62, 64
Holmes, George, 35; quoted, 36–38, 40
Home Rule, 123
Home Rule Bill (1886), 124
Home Rule Bill (1892), 124
Home Rule Bill (1912), 124
Hope, James, quoted, 99
Humbert, General Joseph Amable, 107, 108, 109

Index

Indomptable, the, 62, 63
Ireland Act (1949), 165
Ireton, General, 25, 30
Irish Catholic Confederacy (1642), 15, 16
Irish Citizen Army, 129, 131, 134, 137
Irish Confederation (1847), 116
Irish Free State, 164, 165
Irish nationalism, growth of, 12, 14, 123, 124
Irish National Volunteers, 126, 127
Irish Republican Army, 152, 153, 157, 165
Irish Republican Brotherhood, 118, 126, 127, 129
Irish Suffrage Society, 140
Irish Volunteers (1778), 60
Irish Volunteers (1916), 127, 128, 133, 136, 137, 138, 139

Jackson, Charles, quoted, 71-73, 76-78, 91-92
Jacob, Dr, 73, 76
Jacob's Biscuit Factory, Dublin, 134, 143
James I, King, 4, 7
James II, King, v, 35, 37, 42, 44, 46, 47, 52, 53
Jervis Street Hospital, Dublin, 155
Johnson, Maj.-Gen. Henry, 79, 82, 85, 93

Kelly, John, 80, 81
Kent, Edmund (see Ceannt, Eamonn)
Keogh, Capt Matthew, 74, 75, 97

Kildare, County, 71
Kilkenny, Statutes of, 4
Kilkenny, Assembly of, 10, 11, 12, 19
Killala, 107, 108, 109
Kilmainham Jail, Dublin, 161, 162
Kilwarden, Lord, 114
Kingsborough, Lord, 76
Kingstown, 134, 144
Kinsale, 6

Lake, Lt.-Gen. Gerard, 67, 92, 93, 97
Lalor, James Finton, 118
Lancers, 132
Larne, 126
Lecky, W. E. H., quoted, 91
Leinster, 98
Leinster Committee (Directory) of United Irishmen, 68
Lenthall, the Hon. William, 21
Lewines, Edward, 65
Liberty Hall, Dublin, 137, 139
Limerick, Siege of, 48-52
Limerick, Treaty of, 52, 57
Linenhall Barracks, Dublin, 149
Londonderry, siege, 35-40
Louis XIV, King, 35, 52
Lowe, Brig.-Gen. W. H. M., 141, 156-159
Ludlow, General, 25, 30

MacCracken, Henry Joy, 99
MacDermott, Sean, 130, 131, 156, 160, 162
MacDiarmada, Sean (see MacDermott, Sean)

Index

MacDonagh, Thomas, 130, 131, 134, 160
MacLaren, Archibald, quoted, 89–91
MacMurrough, Dermot, 3
MacNeill, Eoin, 127, 136, 153; quoted, 128
Magazine Fort, Phoenix Park, 137
Mallin, Michael, 134, 141
Manifesto, Pearse's, 152–153
Markievicz, Countess Constance, 141, 158, 159
Marrowbone Lane Distillery, Dublin, 134
Mary, Queen, 6
Mary, Queen of Scots, 6
Maxwell, General Sir John, 162
Mayo, County, 13
Meagher, Thomas Francis, 116, 118; quoted, 117
Meath, County, 67
Mellows, Liam, 134, 161
Mitchell, John, 116, 117, 118
Moira, Lord, 100, 102
Moore, Maj.-Gen. (Sir) John, quoted, 95–97
Moore Street, Dublin, 151, 155–158
Mountjoy, Lord, 6, 79, 81, 84, 100
Mountjoy, the, 39
Mullholland, Captain, quoted, 16–19, 27–30
Munro, General Robert, 11, 14, 16, 17
Munroe, Harry, 100, 106
Munster, 6, 15
Murphy, Father John, 68

Murphy, Father Michael, 90–91
Nathan, Sir Matthew, 136, 142, 162
Nation, The, 116
Nationalist Parliamentary Party, 126
National Literary Society, 124
New Ross, 69, 78, 79–88, 92, 94, 100
Newtownards, 100, 101
Nolan, Loo, 145
Northern Ireland Parliament, 164, 165
Northumberland Road, Dublin, 144
Norway, Hamilton, 134, 135, 136, 149
Norway, Nevil, (Nevil Shute), 134, 135
Norway, Mrs, quoted, 134–136, 144, 149–150

O'Brien, Lt.-Col. Christopher, 10
O'Brien, Murrough, Earl of Inchiquin, 25
O'Brien, Nora Connolly, quoted, 162
O'Brien, William Smith, 116, 117, 118
O'Connell Bridge, Dublin, 140, 147
O'Connell, Daniel, 116
O'Connell Street (see Sackville Street)
O'Donnell, Earl of Tryconnel, 7
O'Farrell, Elizabeth, quoted, 154–155, 156–160

O'Higgins, Brian, quoted, 133–134, 139–140, 141, 146–148, 150–152, 155–156
Old English, 4, 5, 8, 12, 14, 15, 19, 25, 40, 52, 57
Old Irish, 8, 12, 52, 57
O'Mellan, Friar, quoted, 25
O'Neill, Hugh Dubh, 27–30
O'Neill, Hugh, Earl of Tyrone, 6, 7, 13, 14
O'Neill, Lord, 100
O'Neill, Owen Roe, 12, 14, 16, 17, 18, 19, 21, 116
O'Neill, Sir Phelim, 8, 25
O'Rahilly, Michael, (The O'Rahilly), 149, 151, 157, 158
Orangemen, 35, 98
Ormonde, James Butler, 12th Earl of, 11, 14, 19, 21
O'Shea, Kitty, 124
O'Shea, Captain William, 124
Oulart Hill, 68

Pale, the, 4, 14
Palmerstown Park, Dublin, 119
Parnell, Charles Stewart, 123, 124
Parnell Square, Dublin, 140
Parnell Street, Dublin, 152, 157
Pearse, Padraic, 116, 130, 131, 138, 148, 149, 152, 153, 154–161
Pearse, William, 155
Penal Laws, 57–58
Phoenix, the, 39
Pierce, Kathleen, 145
Pitt, William, 61, 113
Pius V, Pope, 6
Plunkett, Joseph, 131, 160
Portobello Barracks, Dublin, 134, 140
Poynings, Edward, 5
Poynings' Law, 5
Presbyterians, 7, 8, 60, 98
Preston, Thomas, 12, 14, 19
Proclamation of the Republic, 129–130
Protestantism, 5, 6, 25
Protestants, 6, 7, 14, 25, 30, 31, 35, 52, 53, 58, 59, 98, 113
Puritans, 6, 7, 25

Randalstown, 99
Redmond, John, 126, 127, 164
Redmond-Howard, Louis George, quoted, 132, 139, 144–146
Reformation, the, v, 4, 5
Restoration, the, 30
Richard II, King, 4
Rinuccini, Giovanni Battista, 15, 16, 19; quoted, 15–16
Roche, Father Philip, 70, 88
Royal College of Surgeons, Dublin, 141
Royal Navy, 127
Ryan, Desmond, quoted, 137–139, 146, 148–149

Sackville Street, Dublin, 128, 129, 133, 140, 147, 150, 160
St. Bartholomew's Day Massacre, 6
St Enda's College, Dublin, 131, 148
Saintfield, 100, 101
St Stephen's Green, Dublin, 133, 134, 135, 141, 142, 143
Sarsfield, Patrick, 40, 48, 52

Index

Schomberg, Duke of, 40, 43-45
Schomberg, Count Meynard, 43-45
Scullabogue, 88, 99
Sheehy-Skeffington, Francis, 140, 141
Shelbourne Hotel, Dublin, 133, 141, 142
Simms, Robert, 99
Simnel, Lambert, 5
Sinn Fein, 126, 164
Sinnott, Colonel Davis, 26
Smith, F. E., 163
Soldier's Song, 148, 164
South Dublin Union, 134, 164
Sow, the Great, 10-11
Spanish Inquisition, 6
Stevens, Lt. John, quoted, 46-47, 50-51
Stoker, E. A., quoted, 128-129
Storey, the Rev. George, quoted, 48-49
Stock, Joseph, Bishop of Killala, 108
Strongbow, Earl of Pembroke, v, 3
Sunday Independent, The, 128
Swift, Jonathan, quoted, 58-59

Taghmon, 96
Talbot, Richard, Earl of Tyrconnell, 35
Tandy, James Napper, 109
Tara, 67, 116
Tecroghan, 21
Temple, Sir John, quoted, 8-9
36th (Ulster) Division, 127
Thomson, James, quoted, 102-105

Three Rocks, 71, 82
Tone, Theobald Wolfe, 61, 107, 108, 109, 116, 163, 165; quoted, 62-66, 98
Tralee Bay, 127
Trim, 20
Trinity College, Dublin, 61, 141, 144

Ulster, v, 7, 11, 16, 17, 41, 98
Ulster Day, 125
Ulster Volunteer Force, 126, 127
Union, Act of, (1800), 113
United Arts Club, Dublin, 143
United Irishmen, Society of, 60, 61, 66-68
United Services Club, Dublin, 149

Vinegar Hill, 69-71, 92-94, 97, 116, 161

Walker, the Rev. George, 35; quoted, 36, 38-40
Waterford, 15, 78
Wentworth, Sir Thomas, 7
Westland Row Railway Station, Dublin, 134
Wexford, 26, 27, 68, 71, 73-78, 96-98
Wexford, County, Rebellion of 1798, 67-98, 100, 107
White, Mrs, quoted, 70-71
Wicklow, County, 13, 71, 89, 93
William III, King, 35, 40-49, 52, 53
Wimborne, Lord, 136

Wood, Anthony, quoted, 24–25
Wood, Thomas, 24
Wren, Sir Christopher, 41

Yeats, W. B., 125, 163
Young, Arthur, quoted, 60
Young Irelanders, 113, 116